Voices of the Land

CANADIAN PLAYS

Series editor: Anne Nothof

This series features a broad range of new Canadian plays that have been professionally produced at least once, with a particular emphasis on the work of playwrights living in Alberta. Publications will include single full-length plays, collections of plays by one playwright, and thematic collections by three or more playwrights. The target audience comprises theatre lovers, actors and playwrights, directors and producers, teachers and students.

VOICES
of the **LAND**

The Seed Savers and Other Plays

Katherine Koller
With an introduction by Anne Nothof

AU PRESS

Copyright © 2012 Katherine Koller
Published by AU Press, Athabasca University
1200, 10011 – 109 Street, Edmonton, AB T5J 3S8

ISBN 978-1-926836-93-5 (print) 978-1-926836-95-9 (PDF) 978-1-926836-94-2 (epub)
A volume in the Canadian Plays series:
ISSN 1917-5086 (print) 1917-5094 (digital)

Cover design by Kate Hall.
Printed and bound in Canada by Marquis Book Printers.

Library and Archives Canada Cataloguing in Publication
Koller, Katherine, 1957–
Voices of the land : the seed savers and other plays /Katherine Koller.

(Canadian plays, ISSN 1917-5086)
Issued also in electronic formats.
ISBN 978-1-926836-93-5

1. Women — Canada, Western — Drama.   2. Canada, Western — Drama.
I. Title.   II. Series: Canadian plays (Edmonton, Alta.)

PS8571.O693V64 2012   C812'.54   C2012-901027-8

Assistance provided by the Government of Alberta, Alberta Multimedia Development Fund.

**Government
of Alberta** ■

We acknowledge the financial support of the Government of Canada through the Canada Book Fund (CBF) for our publishing activities.

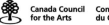

Canada Council   Conseil des Arts
for the Arts   du Canada

To my parents,
who taught me to love the land,
and to all who hear its many voices.

Let them be left, wildness and wet,
Long live the weeds and the wilderness yet.

— GERARD MANLEY HOPKINS,
  "Inversnaid"

Contents

Preface

In each of the four plays in this collection, the land is a central character, with a presence and a voice that interacts with the protagonists. The voice of the land describes the lives of the characters and informs their choices. Natural features of the Canadian prairie environment — the prairie grass in *Cowboy Boots and a Corsage,* the lake in *Abby's Place,* the woods in *The Early Worm Club,* and the wind in *The Seed Savers* — constitute dramatic elements that go beyond setting and backdrop. They are present in the themes and issues, in the conflicts expressed by the characters, and also in the resolutions, effecting transformation through their inherent power.

The action in each play occurs largely or entirely out of doors. This poses the challenge of creating unbounded space within the confines of the theatre through sound, light, stage design, and the suggestive simplicity of a few realistic props. Members of the audience enter an imagined world, bringing with them their own particular relationship to nature. That sensory memory is what I call on when I'm writing, and it's what I need audiences to bring with them when they are participating in the drama. For readers of the plays, that process is even more crucial, because they must connect with their own experiences of the land and imagine new ones: the smell of the prairie grass on the first days of spring, the vocalization of birds in the early morning woods, the silence of the lake at night, interrupted only by the call of the loon, and the sound of the wind in the fields.

The Seed Savers, unlike the other plays, was inspired by an historical event. After reading about the case of Monsanto v. Schmeiser, which by 2004 had reached the Supreme Court of Canada, I decided to go to Bruno, Saskatchewan, to meet Percy and Louise Schmeiser. These folks, farmers for fifty years, were being sued by the Monsanto corporation for growing genetically modified canola in their fields without a license agreement. Monsanto sued on the basis of intellectual property rights: the corporation owns the patent on Roundup Ready Canola, which is resistant to the wide-spectrum herbicide Roundup. This means that farmers can spray this crop to get a weed-free field. The Schmeisers claimed that it was wind, or natural pollination, that had blown the GM canola onto their land. It seemed to me that agriculture was changing — that this case reflected a new way of farming that not everybody welcomed. That's cause for drama, especially when the conflict happens within a family and between neighbours and forces lovers apart. And the wind played a primary role in this drama. I was intrigued by my meeting with the Schmeisers and launched into research about genetics, about the history of canola in Canada, and about corporations like Monsanto. I kept my eye on the legal case, which the Schmeisers ultimately lost in a 5-4 decision, although they were not required to pay damages to the corporation.

Soon my characters began to work with me. This happens most often in the research stage: characters give their names and ask questions that make me look for more material, and then they start challenging each other. I realized, happily, that although I was including certain events that in fact happened to Percy and Louise Schmeiser (the lawsuit, the leather jacket from the company as a reward for information, worldwide speaking engagements), I was not writing a docudrama but a different story about my characters Joe and Mindy, their conflicts, shared desires, and thwarted hopes.

My characters live in my head for a few years, and when they go onto the page, things get increasingly complicated. Now their problems have to fit into a structure and pacing and tempo, and we all go through the process of many drafts, to transform the play to the stage. In the case of the Edmonton premiere of *The Seed Savers*, Michael Clark, artistic director at Workshop West Theatre, showed us the way through. Before the final draft of the play was completed, he and I talked with April Viczko, lighting and set designer, about the nature of the wind as a character. In the end, the wind was evoked by the sheer open space of the stage, surrounded by a single row of chairs placed on a floor painted like the prairie as you see it from the sky. Telephone poles, diminishing in size, were suspended from the ceiling, diagonally across the two-storey headspace, creating perspective and distance. The characters moved through this exposed landscape. Sound designer Paul Morgan Donald created an overlapping aural montage with music and natural sounds emitted from all four corners of the stage area. For me, the audience surrounding the stage became the energy of the wind in that production. In a later production at the Station Arts Centre in Rosthern, Saskatchewan, also directed by Michael Clark, the set by necessity was more contained, but the wind was still there. The audience brought it in with them, along with the yellow of July canola, and their sensory experiences as people of the prairies.

These plays are also linked by their rootedness in the prairies, particularly in Alberta. Although *The Seed Savers* was inspired by the Schmeiser case in Saskatchewan, it could have taken place in Alberta, which is also painted in canola. *Cowboy Boots and a Corsage* comes from a place in southern Alberta, the Milk River Ridge. I can see it in my mind's eye now: the colours of the shortgrass prairie, the roll of the land toward the river, and the wind, the heat, the magic of that untouched virgin prairie. *The Early Worm Club* is set in a boreal forest near Edmonton. I can smell the trembling aspens and balsam poplars and black spruce, and the spring mushrooms. *Abby's Place* is set at a deep and quiet lake in northern Alberta, frequented by white pelicans, redwing blackbirds, and goldfinches. These plays are about places I know and love, and they all look like Alberta. There's a hopeful time-lessness in that, for me. As Abby says in *Abby's Place*, "There will always be the lake," and Mindy says in *The Seed Savers*, "Nature has us all in her hand." The connections made in these plays depend on the land that endures to show us who we are.

— KATHERINE KOLLER

Acknowledgements

These plays were written with the steady support of my husband, Lorne, the Alberta Foundation for the Arts, the Alberta Playwrights Network, and the Banff Centre. My thanks also go to all the theatres, crews, actors, and directors who contributed to the growth of the work in every workshop and production. I am grateful, in particular, for the support of Anne Nothof, Hope McIntyre, and Michael Clark. Production photographs are courtesy of the *Edmonton Journal*, Sarasvàti Productions and FemFest, Workshop West Theatre, and Station Arts Centre. The cover art is from the watercolour rendering of the floor design created by April Viczko for the premiere of *The Seed Savers*.

Katherine Koller's Prairie Synergism
Women on the Land

Voices of the Land brings into the present a long tradition of Canadian prairie plays by women that enact the synergistic relationship of place and person. The landscape acts upon the protagonist in both antagonistic and supportive ways. It may be the occasion for struggle, but also of redemption. It can be both debilitating and energizing in the heroine's journey toward self-affirmation. As in the prairie plays of Gwen Pharis Ringwood, Elsie Park Gowan, Sharon Pollock, Joanna McClelland Glass, and Connie Gault, in Katherine Koller's works the Canadian wilderness resists the idealization of the pastoral motif: a withdrawal from society into an isolated, unspoiled natural environment in order to refresh the spirit and stimulate the imagination. Her Western Canadian protagonists learn to embrace the landscape's terrible beauty and power in the process of discovering their own strengths.

This perspective is also evident in W.O. Mitchell's early plays and novels, and particularly in Wallace Stegner's *Wolf Willow* (1968), where the prairie landscape is present as a defining condition of life — endlessly changing but timeless, adversarial but mind-expanding:

> Desolate? Forbidding? There was never a country that in its good moments was more beautiful. Even in drouth or dust storm or blizzard it is the reverse of monotonous, once you have submitted to it with all of the senses. You don't get out of the wind, but learn to lean and squint against it. You don't escape sky and sun, but wear them in your eyeballs and on your back. You become acutely aware of yourself. The world is very large, the sky even larger, and you are very small. But also the world is flat, empty, nearly abstract, and in its flatness you are a challenging upright thing, as sudden as an exclamation mark, as enigmatic as a question mark.
>
> It is a country to breed mystical people, egocentric people, perhaps poetic people. But not humble ones. (8)

Sharon Butala's portrait of the Saskatchewan prairie evokes the synergism of place and person even more graphically. In *The Perfection of the Morning* (1994), she suggests that a woman's inclination is to make connections with the physical landscape and to evoke a spiritual geography: "And what about the end of the day when in the wash of golden light all blemishes fade and disappear and peace descends over the yellow grasses and the luminous sky? Then, too, there is such perfection that all desire for heaven is absorbed in the glowing, fragile plains, the radiant hills" (190).

The prairie landscape in Katherine Koller's plays is closely associated with the lives of women. The four plays in this collection portray women in terms of a rural environment: their lives are conditioned by the land, which provides a touchstone for values, emotions, and self-awareness. Mindy, in *The Seed Savers*, listens to the wind in order to understand her place in the world: "They say the northwest wind makes you wise" (119). Her husband Joe's response is more pragmatic: the wind may bring intimations of rain; but he is also deeply rooted in the soil. As he explains to his granddaughter, Sky:

> I live close to life. I grow my own seed. I work near the animals, and the birds. They tell me when a storm is coming, by how they move. The hand of nature pushes me, always, to get the jobs done that need doing. I fix machines, keep the equipment running. For the promise I make to the seed. I'm a part of all this, an old guy like. Suits me right down to the ground. (128)

Joe's young neighbour, Solo, has a more intuitive relationship with the land. As they gaze out on the prairie from the narrow ridge of land that functions as his "dream bed," he tells Sky that "when you can see forever like this, you can see inside yourself" (150).

Returning "home" to the farm from Toronto, Sky imagines the prairie as a garden in the biblical *Song of Songs*, its erotic life awakened by the wind:

> *Awake, O North wind, and come thou South!*
> *Blow upon my garden that its spices may flow out.*
> *Awake, O North wind, and come thou South!*
> *Blow upon my garden.*
> *Let my beloved come to his garden,*
> *and eat its choicest fruits.* (161)

In Koller's plays, it is not only the women who are in tune with their environment, however. In her epic history of coal mining in southern Alberta, *Coal Valley: The Making of a Miner,* the young boy Chip hears the voice of the land through the words of an old miner: "It pays to listen. You gotta train your ears, 'cause there's no echo here. The walls absorb sound, muffle it. Like a thick blanket. Like a womb. It pays to listen to her. Right that there. Because Mother Nature, well, she's bigger 'n you, son" (433).

Koller's plays construct the land as both nurturing and destructive. It exacts a high price in physically and mentally wrenching toil, which inevitably conditions the lives of those who persevere or fail. As in Sharon Pollock's *Generations* (1980), *The Seed Savers* enacts the convictions of women who opt to stay on the land, despite the hardships, because it embodies for them a larger purpose: their lives are wholly conditioned by their particular place. For Margaret Nurlin, the mother and wife in *Generations,* whose father lost his farm in the Depression, losing oneself in the work of a prairie farm means being part of something bigger than self-sufficiency. In *The Seed Savers* Mindy, who hangs onto her husband "like the prairie holds down the hills" (190) and who has spent fifty years of her life married to a farmer and a farm, carries her convictions into a wider world, in order to preserve her family's integrity and the health of future generations.

As in Ringwood's *A Fine Coloured Easter Egg,* set in the 1950s, where oil exploration threatens the traditional life of a farm family, Koller's plays may also assume environmental implications, particularly in *The Seed Savers,* as market forces pressure farmers to buy genetically modified seed. In *Cowboy Boots and a Corsage,* the female protagonist resists selling her land; it is the last vestige of untilled and unspoiled prairie and, for her, a place of connection.

Women's prairie plays are often focused on social and family history in terms of landscape: events past, present, and future are conditioned by environment. For example, Elsie Park Gowan's *Breeches from Bond Street* (1949) performs the history of a late-nineteenth-century prairie town through the reformation of a remittance man by a rejected mail-order bride. In *Mirage* (1979), Ringwood shows how communities develop through interdependence and reconciliation between individual and environment. The history of three generations of a prairie family is dramatized as a process, beginning with struggle and near defeat. Family dissolution and despair during the Depression are graphically evoked in Joanna McClelland Glass's *Canadian Gothic* (1972). As are many of her later plays, *Canadian Gothic* is based on memories of her childhood in

Saskatchewan, depicting the emotionally debilitating consequences of living in isolation on the prairies and the conflict between a repressive father and his free-spirited wife and daughter. *Play Memory* (1983) returns to a bleak prairie landscape in rural Saskatchewan during the Depression, portraying an authoritarian father's attempts to control his wife and daughter, with tragic consequences.

Kelly Rebar's *Bordertown Cafe* (1989) also considers the generational prairie family dynamic and the struggle of the younger generation to determine where is "home." Set on the Canadian side of the Alberta-Montana border, it dramatizes the family complexities inherited by a seventeen-year-old boy and his divided loyalties to, and frustrations with, his divorced mother and father. The stage directions signal the radical discrepancy between the claustrophobic, limiting environment of the café and the openness and freedom of the prairie: "*The closed, tight space of the cafe is contrasted by a sense of overwhelming prairie sky that surrounds the set*" (11). In the end, the boy opts to stay in Alberta and help his grandfather with the combining, clearly establishing that his home is on the prairie.

The family dynamic in Koller's plays is similarly portrayed in terms of connection to the land. In *The Seed Savers*, Joe and Mindy's only son has fled to the city to escape the torment occasioned by the "demented wind" (162) and has died there, his ashes "scattered in a city ravine" (123). But his daughter, Sky, returns to find her place in the prairie landscape and in the family: "*Sky takes in the colours, the sounds and smells of fall on the farm. She lets the wind play in her hair, her face, lifts her arms and gives in to it. For the first time in a long time, she's home*" (125). In *Cowboy Boots and a Corsage*, the daughter is tempted to leave her widowed mother, Jeannie, for life in the city with her boyfriend but changes her mind when she visits the crumbling ancestral homestead in the moonlight. She compares Jeannie to the "tough grass" (36) of the untilled prairie, when she finally inherits her mother's determination not to sell out her history. The play's focus is on the land as it participates in the identification of a place called "home."

Beyond their social implications, Koller's plays in this collection have a mythic dimension. As in the prairie plays of Saskatchewan writer Connie Gault, *Sky* (1989) and *The Soft Eclipse* (1990), there is a recognition and acceptance of the extremes of light and shadow that characterize prairie life. The isolation of the landscape may offer respite from predation or intrusion, as in *The Early Worm Club*, or it may provide the means by which a reconciliation with place and people may be achieved. The prairie is place where there is nothing at all, or it may offer the whole wide world — a place to lose or to find oneself. There is no nostalgia, no romanticization, but an acute awareness of the stark contrasts of the prairie landscape, the sudden shifts in light, colour, mood, and season. There is also an awareness of the interconnectedness of place and person, the synergism of landscape and character. In *The Early Worm Club*, although the action is driven by Millie's determination to get a mate, the resolution is achieved in her sense of belonging to the Alberta parkland, with its full spectrum of birdlife.

This awareness of a mythic connection is often voiced by a "seer" figure in prairie literature and drama — Jake in Mitchell's *Jake and the Kid*, for example, or the diviner, Dowser Ringgo, in Ringwood's *Mirage*, who voices an awareness of how the "gods of the land" inform human life. In the Prologue, Dowser invokes an animate and metaphysical landscape:

> A prairie vision must inform my song.
> Much that I count as beautiful or strong
> I learned here, long ago,
> Here in this central plain where my world began
> Stretching out wide and far
> Under the high dome of wheeling stars.

> What gods I knew
> Rose in plumes of dust at high bright noon
> Or flattened themselves on the long shadows
> Or morning and evening on the prairie.
> Phantoms in drifting snow howled with the blizzard,
> Etched mandalas on the window pane
> In the stillness of late dawn when it seemed
> The world would crack apart with cold.

> . . . .

> No easy gods, and yet they challenge, crying "hunt us down,
> Uncover us from beneath your monuments of wood and stone,
> Come, dance and sing with us,
> For without us you are homeless.
> Hunt us down for without us you are forever homeless." (490)

Similarly, in Sharon Pollock's *Generations*, the land has mythic dimensions. As Pollock stipulates in her description of the play's setting: *"There should be some sense of the omniscient presence and mythic proportion of* THE LAND *in the design. . . . During the action of the play, the sun is slowly passing overhead; the earth is turning; this is reflected subtly in the changing patterns of light and shadow"* (610). Like Ringwood, she voices the spirit of place through a prairie seer, Old Eddy, defined by critic Richard Perkyns as "an essential part of the inscrutable landscape" (Introduction to *Generations* 604). As an early pioneer and patriarch of the Nurlin family, Old Eddy has struggled to survive on the prairie and has lost a wife and son, but over time the prairie has become an integral part of his psyche. His passionate attachment to the land is inherited by his grandson, David, who finds it difficult to articulate his feelings to his urbanite girlfriend: "Out *there* . . . is . . . something — I know it. Out there . . . is a feelin' . . . you don't get other places. Other places it's hidden in all the dinky scenery, but on the *prairies* it's just *there*. A *power* . . ." (654).

In *Abby's Place* the seer figure is evident in the self-taught philosopher Clyde, overseer of the village dump, who functions as the guardian spirit of the place. But it is Abby, the dying visitor, who becomes most closely attuned to landscape, forming a spiritual bond with the lake, which she believes will always be there, long after she is gone. As she tries to explain to her husband, Rodney: "I promise that if there is any way of reaching you, this is where I'll be. In the morning, when you go out on the dock to greet the lake, you can wave at me, and I'll wave back" (98). The lake is a place of healing for her husband after her death.

Koller's plays move beyond the confines of the page and the stage in an expression of the personal, social, and mythic dynamics of the prairie landscape. In striking new ways, they focus on the land and on those who live in intimate terms with the land. They dramatize the lives of women who have learned to celebrate the terrible beauty of their environment and have formed a mental and emotional synergism with the prairie.

— ANNE NOTHOF

WORKS CITED

Butala, Sharon. *The Perfection of the Morning: An Apprenticeship in Nature*.
    Toronto: Harper Perennial, 1995.

Gault, Connie. *Sky*. Winnipeg: Blizzard, 1989.

————. *The Soft Eclipse*. Winnipeg: Blizzard, 1990.

Gowan, Elsie Park. *The Hungry Spirit: Selected Plays and Prose*. Ed. Moira Day.
    Edmonton: NeWest Press, 1992.

Koller, Katherine. *Coal Valley: The Making of a Miner*. In *The Alberta Advantage:*
    An Anthology of Plays. Ed. Anne Nothof. Toronto: Playwrights Canada
    Press, 2008.

Pollock, Sharon. *Generations*. In *Major Plays of the Canadian Theatre*. Ed.
    Richard Perkyns. Toronto: Irwin, 1984.

Rebar, Kelly. *Bordertown Cafe*. Winnipeg: Blizzard, 1989.

Ringwood, Gwen Pharis. *The Collected Plays of Gwen Pharis Ringwood*. Ed.
    Enid Delgatty Rutland. Ottawa: Borealis Press, 1982.

Stegner, Wallace. *Wolf Willow*. Toronto: Macmillan, 1968.

Voices of the Land

Cowboy Boots and a Corsage, Edmonton Fringe Festival: Joan Hurley as Jeannie; Clare Denman as Roxanne; John Weed as Paul; Barbara Schmid as Angelina. Photo by Ed Kaiser.

COWBOY BOOTS
and a CORSAGE

Cowboy Boots and a Corsage was first produced at the Edmonton Fringe Festival in August 1991 with the following cast and crew:

JEANNIE Joan Hurley
ROXANNE Clare J. Denman
ANGELINA Barbara Schmid
PAUL / WELFARE AGENT / HARRY John Weed
MUSICIAN Blake Winnipeg

DIRECTOR Jonathan Christenson
STAGE MANAGER Sian Williams
DRAMATURGE Patricia Badir
SET Maureen Harvey
COSTUMES Brigitte Blunck de Vicque
CARPENTER Lorne Wensel
SPECIAL EFFECTS Robert Koller

The script was slightly revised for a production at FemFest! by Sarasvàti Productions in Winnipeg from 7 to 15 June 2003 with the following cast and crew:

JEANNIE Cairn Moore
ROXANNE Andrea Dziadek
ANGELINA Alison Kolisnyk
PAUL Illya Torres-Garner
WELFARE / REAL ESTATE AGENT Henri Marcoux
HARRY Darryl Miller

DIRECTOR Hope McIntyre
DRAMATURGE Joanna Falck
MUSIC Illya Torres-Garner

Characters

JEANNIE, newly widowed, in her forties
ROXANNE, her daughter, in Grade 12
PAUL, Roxanne's boyfriend, also in Grade 12, plays the guitar music bridges
  where indicated
WELFARE AGENT, male, who also plays REAL ESTATE AGENT
HARRY, in his forties
ANGELINA, Paul's mother, in her forties

Set

There are three main playing areas: the half-section, where Jeannie goes in her
mind; at stage right, a table and two chairs — Jeannie's kitchen; at stage left,
an area representing various locales in town, Roxanne's space.

Music

For bridges between scenes, and especially to underscore Jeannie's time on
the land, Paul plays acoustic guitar. He also sings the Grad song.

SCENE 1   Jeannie's Kitchen

Music.
Jeannie, in her mind, is at her land, where she retreats often. Angelina is seated
at the table, set with two cups, a deck of cards, and a cribbage board. Angelina
has a tote bag. Jeannie carries a bottle of amaretto.

JEANNIE   (*To the cows*) What are you looking at? Hey, Lola! Matilda!
            Trudy! It's just me. Just me. I need you girls more than
            ever now. I wish I could just stand there and watch,
            like you! You big smart asses!

Angelina sneezes. Jeannie brings a bottle of amaretto to the table.

JEANNIE   Hot tea for your hay fever.

ANGELINA   Oh, thanks, Jeannie. It's worse this spring.

JEANNIE   Then let's make it blueberry tea.

ANGELINA   Oh, no . . . ah, blueberry for me, please.

JEANNIE   Okey-dokey. Clear for you, double blue for me.

ANGELINA   That stuff costs the earth. Can you really afford it, I mean —

JEANNIE   Don't get your tits in a knot. I found this in the closet. I
            think it was a present. An anniversary present. I thought
            we should pause to celebrate. Since you're here.

ANGELINA   Well, it's a good thing I came by. To keep you company.

JEANNIE   And ask me something. You always do. So what's on
            your mind, Angelina?

ANGELINA   I was just wondering if you got your insurance claim yet.

JEANNIE   Ha! He never bought insurance in his life.

ANGELINA   I thought so.

Jeannie reaches for more amaretto.

JEANNIE   Happy Anniversary.

ANGELINA   You could probably do without this.

Angelina corks the bottle.

JEANNIE I couldn't.

ANGELINA Well, honestly, Jeannie, here it is only three months after your husband drops dead at Harry's Bar and Billiards and you're soaking up the sauce in your tea!

JEANNIE Oh, dry up, Angelina. Play cards.

ANGELINA My crib. Fifteen two, fifteen four, and eight's a dozen.

JEANNIE Why do we bother playing? We know you're going to finish first. You're always first. First to get asked out, first to get knocked up, first to get married . . .

ANGELINA Not first to get widowed, that's you.

JEANNIE Thank heavens I get to be first at something.

ROXANNE *(off)* I'm home!

ANGELINA If you don't watch out, you're going to be first at something else.

Roxanne enters kitchen.

JEANNIE I know what you're thinking. Technically, that would be a tie.

ANGELINA Over my dead body.

JEANNIE *(Concentrating on her cards)* Hi, honey.

ANGELINA Hello, Roxanne.

ROXANNE Howdy.

JEANNIE How was school?

ROXANNE Got a detention.

ANGELINA Oh!

ROXANNE Smoking in the can.

JEANNIE Smoking in the can.

Jeannie slips away to the land.

JEANNIE	Remember we used to do that, Ange? That was before you had hay fever, of course. And it wasn't in the can, it was under the school steps.
ROXANNE	Anything to eat around here?
ANGELINA	Oh, I brought some of my pound cake for you two. It's fresh baked!
ROXANNE	How wholesome.
JEANNIE	You had your eye on Charlie even then. Even though he was looking at me.
ANGELINA	One of Paul's favourites.
ROXANNE	Pound cake?

Roxanne reads Angelina's cards, then takes up Jeannie's.

JEANNIE	You knew exactly how you were going to fix things. One, two —
ROXANNE	Four, six, eight and his nibs is one more!
ANGELINA	Paul loves all kinds of baked goods. Whoever marries him will be in the kitchen all day long.
ROXANNE	Ha! The Paul I know likes his sweet stuff any way he can find it.
ANGELINA	I wonder, Roxanne, if you've given any thought to a summer job.
ROXANNE	I might do some babysitting. I like kids.
ANGELINA	Maybe I could find you some work on a farm, so you could see what it's like.
ROXANNE	I can see what that's like. All I have to do is look at you.
ANGELINA	Your poor mother. With a girl like you.

Music.
Paul enters, guitar in hand. Jeannie moves to kitchen to answer phone.

PAUL	Hi, it's me.

JEANNIE	Hi, kiddo.
PAUL	Roxy home?
JEANNIE	Yeah, she's here. Playin' cards.
PAUL	Shoot. Is my Ma there, too?
ANGELINA	Is that Paul?
JEANNIE	Yes, sir.
PAUL	Don't let on it's me.
JEANNIE	How come?
PAUL	She'll think up more stuff for me to do, and I . . . wanted to come by and see Roxy tonight.
ROXANNE	Is he coming over?
JEANNIE	Only if you keep your shirt on, buster.
ANGELINA	Is that Paul?

Jeannie nods at Roxanne.

PAUL	Oh, yeah. Ha. That was . . . ha, ha. Okay. See ya.
JEANNIE	Later. Bye.

Paul exits.

ROXANNE	Gotta go wash the car. Toss the niner, Mom.

Roxanne takes pound cake, exits.

ANGELINA	I don't know what I would do if I were you, Jeannie. At her age, Roxy needs things.
JEANNIE	As long as she's got gas money, she doesn't complain.
ANGELINA	My Paul says your Roxanne is getting wilder every day, racing around in that car.
JEANNIE	Yeah? Your Paul ought to know. Caught the two of them the other day . . . starting to strip down from the heat. They had the windows fogged up, but I know where he's got his tattoo!

ANGELINA	Well, all I know is, if Roxanne can't find what she needs at home, she'll go looking for it elsewhere.
JEANNIE	Like you did.
ANGELINA	That was a long time ago.
JEANNIE	You think Roxanne would get herself into trouble on purpose?
ANGELINA	Like you say, it's been done before. My Paul doesn't need any accident with some girl right now! He's got plans!
JEANNIE	Then maybe you should talk to him!
ANGELINA	I'm just worried about you, Jeannie. I don't know how you're going to manage, with house and car payments, and all your other expenses.
JEANNIE	Are you the one who made the call? Ange?
ANGELINA	Nine, ten, eleven . . . I'm out!

Welfare Agent enters, looks around as if inspecting Jeannie's land, carries file folder. Jeannie tries to block him.

JEANNIE	What do you want?
AGENT	Well, Ma'm, we've checked your file, but there's a problem with support because you own a certain half-section of land.
JEANNIE	My mother willed it to me.
AGENT	With the half-section, you are ineligible.
JEANNIE	But . . .
AGENT	There is a way around this problem. Heh, heh. Don't tell anyone I suggested it, but what I usually tell my clients is, sell the pile of rocks 'n weeds, spend the money and reapply!
JEANNIE	No way.
AGENT	Then, sorry. Can't help you, toodeloo.

Agent exits as Roxanne enters. Jeannie comes back to the kitchen.

ROXANNE	Mom?
JEANNIE	We're not taking any money from them.
ROXANNE	Who?
ANGELINA	The welfare, that's who.
JEANNIE	Bunch of clowns. Just because I own a few handfuls of prairie grass.
ANGELINA	Well, Jeannie, you know I could get Charlie to buy it!
ROXANNE	Unload it, Mom.
JEANNIE	No!
ANGELINA	You've let him graze our cattle on it for years!
JEANNIE	I like your cows.
ANGELINA	Then at least let Charlie buy it, Jeannie. You could still . . . use it.
JEANNIE	I won't sell.
ANGELINA	Why not?
ROXANNE	We need the money, Mom.
JEANNIE	You don't have any land of your own. You wouldn't know what it's like.

Jeannie moves to the land.

ANGELINA	I don't suppose I would.
ROXANNE	What's the big deal?
ANGELINA	I've never really thought about it. I mean, the house is mine, and the farm is Charlie's. It's that simple.
ROXANNE	It's pasture.
ANGELINA	Well, I better run along. Going up to Lethbridge tomorrow to get my boys outfitted for Paul's graduation.
ROXANNE	It's just grass.
ANGELINA	By the way, Roxanne, have you made plans for Grad yet?
ROXANNE	No. Not really. I don't know.

ANGELINA	We're putting on a dinner dance down at the legion hall.
ROXANNE	Hey, Mom.
ANGELINA	Maybe you don't go in for all that.
ROXANNE	I haven't thought about it. Mom?
ANGELINA	Then what?
ROXANNE	Summer! Parties, swimming, barbeques . . .
ANGELINA	And after that?
ROXANNE	I don't know! How should I know? I'm just a kid!

Roxanne exits.

ANGELINA	I feel sorry for you, Jeannie. Listen, are you sure he didn't put away something in stocks or bonds? You know how men are. They buy stuff, sock it away somewhere and pretty near forget. . . . Jeannie? Oh, Jeannie!

Angelina exits. Music.

JEANNIE	There was one bond. I had Elmer down at the bank check on it. He said it was cashed three years ago. He gave me the exact date. Round about spring thaw. Day like today. You would have thought the smell of spring on the prairie would have been enough to lift anyone's spirits. The way I figure it, Harry's Bar and Billiards must have made a bundle that March.

Jeannie exits.

SCENE 2   School Parking Lot

Roxanne and Paul enter, flirting and horsing around. She tries to steal his soccer ball. Paul has his guitar.

ROXANNE	Hey, I was wondering about Grad.
PAUL	What about it?

ROXANNE	It's going to be a big deal this year, eh?
PAUL	Gotta be, with Ma running it.
ROXANNE	Well . . . are we going or what?
PAUL	I am. My Ma's got me doing the Grad song. She's wound up like an eight-day clock. You'd think it was her Grad.
ROXANNE	So you're going with your Ma.
PAUL	Well . . . it's mostly for people who are passing the year.
ROXANNE	Yeah, so?
PAUL	Well, you hang out a lot at school.
ROXANNE	I mostly go there to smoke.
PAUL	Yeah, well, I didn't think you'd be going to Grad.
ROXANNE	But you are.
PAUL	Getting my Grade 12 means getting four wild years in Calgary.
ROXANNE	I'd like to go, too.
PAUL	You would?
ROXANNE	To Grad.
PAUL	Yeah? It could be a really fun time.
ROXANNE	Yeah, maybe.
PAUL	We'd make a pretty good-looking couple.
ROXANNE	You going to wear one of those tuxedos?
PAUL	What about you? Have I ever seen you in a dress?
ROXANNE	Just that once. At the service for my Dad.
PAUL	Yeah, but even then you wore your boots.
ROXANNE	Yeah, I did.
PAUL	For Grad, you'd have to leave them at home.
ROXANNE	Oh, yeah?
PAUL	Yeah. Okay. I'll tell you what. You pass, and I'll take you to Grad.

| ROXANNE | Maybe I will, maybe I won't. |
| PAUL | It's your funeral. |

Paul throws the ball at Roxanne. Music. Roxanne picks up her knapsack and crosses to the kitchen.

SCENE 3 Kitchen / Harry's Bar

Roxanne kicks the ball.

JEANNIE	Roxy? Where were you?
ROXANNE	Out driving.
JEANNIE	With Paul?
ROXANNE	Yeah.
JEANNIE	What's new with him?
ROXANNE	Not much. He's been talking about Grad.
JEANNIE	Oh.
ROXANNE	It's probably a bunch of crap.
JEANNIE	I don't know.
ROXANNE	Well, you went to yours, didn't you?
JEANNIE	No.
ROXANNE	Why not?
JEANNIE	I was honeymooning.
ROXANNE	But you got your Grade 12.
JEANNIE	He did. He was finished a year ahead of me.
ROXANNE	He did and you didn't.
JEANNIE	He wanted to go camping in the foothills as soon as it was warm enough to go with no tent.
ROXANNE	No tent?

JEANNIE	Slept under the stars every night.
ROXANNE	It never rained?
JEANNIE	No.
ROXANNE	Sounds like Dad all right. Always taking chances.
JEANNIE	I took a chance, too. He didn't talk me into quitting. I just did it. I wanted him.
ROXANNE	So you don't have your high school.
JEANNIE	They're asking for it everywhere: the bank, the Saan store, the lodge, the hospital . . .
ROXANNE	But everyone in town knows you.
JEANNIE	That's what makes it worse.
ROXANNE	So what are you going to do?
JEANNIE	I'm going to have to sell —
ROXANNE	It's about time.
JEANNIE	— the car.
ROXANNE	Not the car! Dad bought it for us!
JEANNIE	It's not paid for yet. It's costing me.
ROXANNE	But I love that car! I mean, it's a car, not an old dusty pickup! And I've been taking really good care of it!
JEANNIE	I know.
ROXANNE	We need the car.
JEANNIE	I don't really see why when we live in a town where everything is in walking distance.
ROXANNE	That's why we need it. To go other places.

Harry enters, sets bar.

JEANNIE	(*Pause*) There's a sign up at Harry's Bar and Billiards.
ROXANNE	I saw it. "Help Wanted."

JEANNIE	As if I'd ever want to help Harry.
ROXANNE	It wasn't Harry's fault.
JEANNIE	You want me to go work in a bar?
ROXANNE	I don't know.
JEANNIE	The same bar that killed your Dad?
ROXANNE	If you have to.
JEANNIE	I'm not going anywhere near the place.
ROXANNE	Then maybe I should go work for Harry.
JEANNIE	Over my dead . . .
ROXANNE	Yeah, well you're half-dead at least. How could you go out talking to people with nails like this? You're a mess.
JEANNIE	Oh, who cares?
ROXANNE	I'll get the kit. I'll be right back.

Roxanne exits. Music. Jeannie gets up, slowly goes to the land.

JEANNIE	I've been to Harry's often enough, eh? It got so he and I had a code. He'd phone me and say —
HARRY	Hey, Jeannie!

Roxanne enters.

ROXANNE	Mom?
HARRY	There's someone down here who needs a ride home.
JEANNIE	Right off the rigs, spreading money like wildfire. But other times, when there wasn't much to spend, it could be bad —
HARRY	Hey, Jeannie!
ROXANNE	Where'd you go?
HARRY	You want him or should I call the sheriff?
ROXANNE	Mom?

Roxanne exits with kit.

JEANNIE	And all through everything I kept coming out here, looking for . . . the way it was before. I loved it when he used to say, "Just you and me and the horizon." Now it's just me and you girls. Looking down at the grass. I'm just like you. Can't even hold my head up to look at the sky. Maybe I should just crawl down a hole and pull it in after me.

Jeannie crumples.
Real Estate Agent enters.

AGENT	Your daughter, pretty little thing, she told me I'd find you here. A friend of a friend said this here bit o' land could be up for sale. I could list it for ya. I could sell it today. Money in the bank tomorrow. What do you say?

A pause, then Jeannie moos, low, then louder.

JEANNIE	Nooo!

Agent exits.

	Did you hear what I said, you big, fat cows? Don't stare at me like that! Wish I could chew it away like you. Oh my girls — Lulu, Millicent, Betsy, Geraldine! I don't want to lose you. I don't want to lose this place. What if Harry won't hire me? What would be worse is that the only job I ever get is working for Harry.

Jeannie moves to the bar.

HARRY	I thought you might be calling.
JEANNIE	I need a job.
HARRY	It's hard work. You're on your feet all the time.
JEANNIE	I can handle it.
HARRY	Any experience?
JEANNIE	Cut it out, Harry. Do you want me or not?

HARRY	Skirt looks good, anyway.
JEANNIE	How much?
HARRY	The minimum. But you get your tips. Can't expect a whole lot, though. People are paying big bills. Prices for grain are still down. Machinery's busting left and right. And then there's the damn weather.
JEANNIE	As long as it makes them want to drink more, what do you care, eh, Harry?
HARRY	Ha! I'm not stopping them.
JEANNIE	Just one more thing. It's about Roxanne.
HARRY	How is foxy Roxy?
JEANNIE	She's talking about graduating this year.
HARRY	So what about her?
JEANNIE	If she needs me, I want her to be able to call down to the bar, anytime.
HARRY	Okay, but I don't want her hanging around here.

Harry ties a money apron on Jeannie, taking his time and looking her right over.

| JEANNIE | She won't. |
| HARRY | Need that like a hole in the head. |

Music. Harry hands Jeannie a broom. They exit.

SCENE 4   The Playground

Roxanne enters, holding hands with Paul.

ROXANNE	What a great day! Look at that perfect sky. Makes ya just want to blend in with it.
PAUL	Yeah.
ROXANNE	Feels good to skip school once in a while, eh?

PAUL	Yeah. Spring fever. It gets ya.
ROXANNE	Ever think of just taking off with it?
PAUL	What do you mean?
ROXANNE	Just letting it take over. Packing a bag, jumping in your truck and driving.
PAUL	What?
ROXANNE	Just you and me, driving fast, and the horizon.
PAUL	No!
ROXANNE	Aw, come on!
PAUL	No way, Roxy. Get real! Just because I'm cutting a class doesn't mean I want to run away.
ROXANNE	You're sure?
PAUL	Forget it.
ROXANNE	I forgot. You know exactly where you're going.
PAUL	Yeah. I've thought about it for a long time. I'm doing my degree and then working for my dad. If things go okay, he'll make me a partner in the farm.
ROXANNE	Just like your dad.
PAUL	All your dad gave you is itchy feet.

Roxanne starts to leave.

	Hey, where are you going?
ROXANNE	I don't know . . . and right now I like it that way.
PAUL	Hey, Rox! Wait. I want you to hear this.

Music.
(*Sings*)

Whatever I do, I do
Wherever I go, I go
You gotta know,
it will be with you.

If I stay near
or if I go far,
I'm gonna go
with you in my heart.
Whatever I do, I do
Wherever I go, I go
To find the road
I'll take with you.

Roxanne and Paul exit, together.

SCENE 5 Harry's Bar

Harry is resetting glasses. Jeannie checks a bill, her watch.

HARRY   Hey, Jeannie. That table at the back is looking thirsty again.

JEANNIE   I just took them a round five minutes ago.

HARRY   Charlie's pretty high after his bull won first at the fair today, but his old lady won't let him stay out late. See, Angelina's checking her watch. Go get their order.

JEANNIE   I think Charlie's had enough.

HARRY   I'm the boss.

JEANNIE   Hey, Harry. Charlie's had a good time, and Angelina needs a good lay. Let her take him home in a happy mood.

HARRY   They're leaving. You owe me one.

JEANNIE   Uh, uh, Harry. You got it wrong. You're the one who's in debt. It's the reason you hired me. How many more widows you trying to make, Harry?

HARRY   Can it, Jeannie.

JEANNIE   Enough to open a new bar? Maybe call it Harry's Harum?

HARRY   All I did was pick him up until there was nothing left. Just like you did.

JEANNIE	Excuse me, it's last call. Time to get my tips from those Calgary bigshots.

Jeannie goes to her land and counts money in her pocket.

JEANNIE	Nineteen, twenty . . . thirty . . . sixty-five. Holy cats! Not bad for an old girl, eh?
HARRY	Not bad at all.

Harry gets ready to leave.

JEANNIE	Never thought I'd get anything in a place I lost so much.
HARRY	Hey, Jeannie, if you come home with me, it wouldn't take long to get it all back. You deserve it. Everyone does. Even me.

Roxanne enters kitchen with books.
Harry takes off Jeannie's money apron, lets it drop, turns her around to face him.

JEANNIE	My mother used to say having your own land is having your own nickel. For me, it's having my own history.
HARRY	One day, maybe you'll invite me out there.
JEANNIE	Wouldn't that give the old girls something to chew about?

Music. Jeannie goes to kitchen. Harry exits.

SCENE 6 Kitchen

Roxanne is studying at the table.

ROXANNE	I was wondering when you'd get home.
JEANNIE	What are you doing still up? Was Paul here?
ROXANNE	Nope.
JEANNIE	Did you get some supper?

ROXANNE	Paul invited me to his place.
JEANNIE	How's Angelina?
ROXANNE	Whenever I'm there, she's rattling around like seed in a two-inch wind.
JEANNIE	She likes to fuss. Oh, my feet are so sore they could fall off.
ROXANNE	You should get yourself a pair of cowboy boots.
JEANNIE	When did you start wearing those again?
ROXANNE	Been a while.
JEANNIE	Been since he's gone.
ROXANNE	You can walk forever without getting sore. He was right about that. Here, try them on.
JEANNIE	Okay. Hey, they fit good. You warmed 'em up for me. Nice.
ROXANNE	So . . . decent tips tonight?
JEANNIE	Pretty decent. Why?
ROXANNE	I was wondering about . . . buying a Grad dress.
JEANNIE	How much for a Grad dress?
ROXANNE	The nice ones are pretty expensive.
JEANNIE	Are you going with Paul?
ROXANNE	Yeah, I guess.
JEANNIE	What about parents? Don't parents get to go?
ROXANNE	You want to?
JEANNIE	If you're graduating, I'm going, come hell or high water.
ROXANNE	Then you'll need a dress, too.
JEANNIE	I can't wear the same one?
ROXANNE	No.
JEANNIE	Not in this town.

Angelina enters bar.

ROXANNE	Oh, before I forget, Paul's mom said to remind you about canasta on Thursday afternoon.
JEANNIE	Can't. Gotta work.
ROXANNE	No time for bat club anymore, eh, Mom?
JEANNIE	At Grad, would I have to sit with her?
ROXANNE	Well, yeah. You sit with your date's parents.
JEANNIE	That settles it, then. We need to go shopping.

Music. Jeannie and Roxanne exit.

SCENE 7 Harry's Bar

Harry enters bar.

ANGELINA	Oh, listen, Harry. Could I get a glass of water?
HARRY	You bet.
ANGELINA	Thank you. Oh!
HARRY	What's eating you?
ANGELINA	Oh, those women! You give them simple instructions on how to make paper rosettes and they don't follow unless you're holding their hand! I've been running around town all afternoon!
HARRY	Here, on the house.

Harry serves her a beer.

ANGELINA	In the middle of the day?
HARRY	Don't like to see a lady so agitated.
ANGELINA	Well, thanks. Umm. Now if I didn't have to face that vixen, Roxanne, tonight.

Jeannie enters.

| HARRY | Roxy? |

ANGELINA	She's got my Paul mooning over her like a wet dog. He can't keep his mind on his schoolwork, and exams are just around the corner.
HARRY	He's a smart fella.
ANGELINA	He used to be, before he took up with her. She has her meals at our house most nights, well, because Paul thinks he has to take care of her, now that Jeannie is always here. . . . I tell you, she's lost track of that girl, but I'll be darned if I'm going to let go of my Paul!
JEANNIE	You looking for me?
HARRY	Sight for sore eyes.
ANGELINA	Oh!
JEANNIE	Sorry I'm late.
ANGELINA	Jeannie, can I talk to you about the Grad dance?
JEANNIE	I should get to work.
ANGELINA	I'm just a bit keyed up. They've put me in charge of pretty near everything . . . and there's hardly any time left, so many things to do! What about you? Do you know what you're wearing?
JEANNIE	I'm not sure.
ANGELINA	Me neither. I can't decide between my peach or my dusty rose! Either way, I don't suppose we'll clash, will we, sitting at the same table?
JEANNIE	Don't worry, Ange.
HARRY	Time's a-wasting.
ANGELINA	The other thing is, on top of everything else, Charlie and I are celebrating our anniversary soon, and I thought, why not buy that patch of pasture as my gift to him? What do you think, Jeannie? I've got my cheque book.
JEANNIE	It's the only thing I've got that you don't.
ANGELINA	But it would help you out. You wouldn't have to work here.
HARRY	She likes it here.

JEANNIE	I do.
ANGELINA	Oh! Well! I never knew!
JEANNIE	And you don't have to be feeding Roxy all the time.
ANGELINA	Oh, it's no trouble; when you cook for eight every night, one more doesn't matter. It's just these exams coming up! I'll be glad when that's over. Well, I'll see you on the big night! You're looking good, Jeannie!

Music. Angelina exits. Jeannie exits to the land.
Harry exits, touching Jeannie as he goes.

SCENE 8 Kitchen

Roxanne enters.

ROXANNE	Mom! Where are you?

Jeannie does not respond.

ROXANNE	I wish you wouldn't do this!

Jeannie pushes herself back to the reality of her kitchen, lays out bills, pencil, adds on crib board.

JEANNIE	I'm here.
ROXANNE	Bills?
JEANNIE	One more. It's a biggie.

Jeannie opens envelope.

ROXANNE	For what?
JEANNIE	Taxes. On my half-section.
ROXANNE	But doesn't Paul's dad pay that? He's using it for pasture.
JEANNIE	Nope. Whoever owns it, pays it.
ROXANNE	So, how much is left?

JEANNIE	After the taxes, about a hundred dollars.
ROXANNE	Not much.
JEANNIE	Probably enough for one dress.
ROXANNE	What about tickets, for the dinner dance. And shoes? And a dress for you?
JEANNIE	Maybe I could buy some material and make one.
ROXANNE	Sure, Mom. Like the time I was twelve and I needed a new coat, and you never got past cutting the thing out. The material is still sitting downstairs somewhere!
JEANNIE	This is different. There's a deadline.
ROXANNE	Just when are you going to do it? You're out every night 'til late, and just barely out of your housecoat after school when I get home. And then you're gone to the bar again!
JEANNIE	I'm going there to work.
ROXANNE	Yeah, to make just enough money to pay taxes on your stupid half-section.
JEANNIE	That land is my friend.
ROXANNE	It's more than that! Every time I look for you, you're never here, and even if you are, you're not!
JEANNIE	I haven't been out there since I started work. One of the reasons for that is I need the car to get there. I haven't seen the car — or you — for ages!
ROXANNE	I've been at Paul's. Studying. Really.
JEANNIE	I need to see the sky.

Jeannie starts to move away to the land.

ROXANNE	Okay. Wait, Mom. How about this? How about if we, you and me, how about if we go up to Lethbridge on Sunday, because you don't have to work, right? They've got this mall open on Sundays up there, and we can find some good sales, and get our dresses for Grad?
JEANNIE	You go ahead. I'm not much for crowds.

ROXANNE	What do you mean? Don't you want to go to Grad?
JEANNIE	I'm not spending my land tax money on a petal pink dress to go to Angelina's private party for Paul.
ROXANNE	Hey, it's my Grad, too! I'm going to pass! I'm going to graduate!
JEANNIE	Here. Take the hundred bucks. Your graduation present.
ROXANNE	This is because of a bunch of prairie grass?
JEANNIE	It's just that it's mine. It could be yours some day.
ROXANNE	Well, I'm going to Grad, even if I have to wear my cowboy boots!

Music. Roxanne stuffs the money in her jeans and pulls her boots off Jeannie. Roxanne exits. Jeannie picks up the cards and lets them fall on the table.

SCENE 9 The Land

Roxanne and Paul enter with their arms around each other.

ROXANNE	Just what I thought. Prairie grass and cowpies and flies.
PAUL	Never been tilled. My dad says it's the best for cattle. If you look hard, you can see dozens of species of grass. All with their own purpose. Cattle keep it growin'. Land needs the cattle as much as cattle need the land.
ROXANNE	Huh.
PAUL	You sure aced exams last week. You decide to do something, you really do it.
ROXANNE	Yeah, I beat you in Social, didn't I? What about Biology?
PAUL	You're the one who should go to university.
ROXANNE	I'd have to sell the car.
PAUL	Come visit me in Calgary next year?

ROXANNE	I've got the summer to decide.
PAUL	Ever been to the zoo?
ROXANNE	My Dad was going to take me once, but he never did.
PAUL	I'd take you to the zoo, and then up to the Husky Tower.
ROXANNE	Ha! You're going to be too busy to go to the zoo.
PAUL	I won't know anyone. It's going to be lonely.
ROXANNE	Not for long.
PAUL	Will you write to me?
ROXANNE	Never written anybody any letters before.
PAUL	Hey, Grad pictures are next week. I want a big one of you to take with me to Calgary.
ROXANNE	Really? Okay.
PAUL	I can hardly wait for Grad night. There's an after-party out at the lake. Don't bring your bathing suit, though. We're going to go skinny dipping, eh, Roxy?
ROXANNE	Huh. You see up there on the hill? That's the old homestead.
PAUL	We're going to party all night long.
ROXANNE	It's where my great-grandparents lived.
PAUL	You know, my Dad asked my Ma to marry him on Grad night. Told me he was so pissed he didn't know what he was saying!
ROXANNE	What?
PAUL	Who knows, eh, Roxy? Maybe you'll come up to Calgary and decide you want to stay a while. I'd like that.
ROXANNE	Yeah?
PAUL	Maybe you'll end up with me some day.
ROXANNE	You think so.
PAUL	Let's go for a ride, hey?

ROXANNE	Just a minute, okay?
PAUL	I'll start the car.

Music. Paul exits.

ROXANNE	Hey Paul! I'm driving!

Roxanne runs off.

SCENE 10   Kitchen / Legion Hall

Jeannie enters kitchen in a housecoat as Angelina, in her Grad outfit, enters the Legion Hall. Jeannie brings a bottle of wine and a glass to the table. She mimes an offer of wine to Angelina, who waves her away with last-minute decoration tizzies.

JEANNIE	Hey, Ange. I'm thinking of having some company out at my land one of these nights. In case you see a little campfire out there. Don't worry. It's just a little fire. Nothing I can't handle.

Paul, in his tux, gets checked over by Angelina. Paul makes his way to the kitchen. Angelina watches him go, then exits.

PAUL	Anybody home?
JEANNIE	Don't you look spiffy!
PAUL	I feel like a turkey.
JEANNIE	Hey, Roxy!
PAUL	Sorry you're not coming to Grad.
JEANNIE	You'll have a good time without me.

Roxanne enters carrying boxes.

JEANNIE	You moving out?
ROXANNE	How come you're home?
JEANNIE	I booked the night off, remember? Why aren't you dressed?

ROXANNE	I'm taking out the garbage.
PAUL	I just came over to give you this. I ordered it a long time ago. Remember I asked what colour your dress was? You didn't know, so I got white. Figured white would match with everything. I didn't really want to go at all when you said you weren't. But it means a lot to my Ma, so what the heck. My Dad and I plan on getting plastered.
ROXANNE	Don't.
PAUL	Sorry.
JEANNIE	Rox, what is all this stuff?
ROXANNE	Grades 1 to 11. I can't believe you saved it all. (*Puts on knapsack*) And this is Grade 12.
JEANNIE	Paul, be a honey and load this in the car, will you?
PAUL	Sure.

Paul exits with boxes.

JEANNIE	I need a few things.

Jeannie puts cards in her housecoat pocket.

ROXANNE	What are you doing, Mom?
JEANNIE	Matches . . . what else?
ROXANNE	Mom, where are you going?

Paul enters.

JEANNIE	Kiss Paul goodbye and meet me in the car.

Jeannie exits.

ROXANNE	I gotta go.

Roxanne puts on her jacket.

PAUL	Wait. Let me pin this on for you. There. Yeah. White definitely goes with denim.

ROXANNE	Thanks. See ya.
PAUL	For sure! Hey! This one is for Jeannie!

Music. Roxanne takes it, kisses Paul and exits. Paul takes a drink of the wine left on the table and exits.

SCENE 11   The Land

Music. Roxanne and Jeannie enter with their corsages pinned on. It is dusk. They sing with the music.

JEANNIE AND ROXANNE	*Oh, give me a home, where the buffalo roam, and the deer and the antelope play.*
JEANNIE	Hey, Belle!
ROXANNE	Belle?
JEANNIE	I don't know. I name them all, over and over again. Just try to get that old girl's attention! Hey! I said, Belle!
ROXANNE	Over here, you big ball of blubber!
JEANNIE	Yeah, you! I got company tonight. Yeah, that's right. Time to go home.
ROXANNE	Bye, Belle.
JEANNIE	What's first?

Jeannie lights fire.

ROXANNE	Grade 12! Good riddance.

Roxanne throws paper in the fire, crunching each sheet into a ball. Pause.

ROXANNE	It's pretty quiet out here. Like someone's listening.
JEANNIE	Well, it's alive, you know.
ROXANNE	What?
JEANNIE	The land. Never dies, no matter who walks on it or when. Just like the big round moon.

ROXANNE	Puffed right up for Grad night.
JEANNIE	I used to come out here all the time when I was a little girl. My parents used to bring me over for a weekend. They'd call it "going on a holiday." Then it was just me and Granny and Gramps. Those were the best days.
ROXANNE	This is where you used to go, isn't it? When Dad would get to you.
JEANNIE	Feels good to get out here again. This is my property. Nobody can push me around. Cows are my guests. Good listeners, eh? They just stand there and chew while I'm yelling to kingdom come. Hey, my turn to burn something.

Jeannie flings cards into the fire.

JEANNIE	Never played very well anyhow. I need a new hobby. Knitting, maybe.
ROXANNE	You, knitting? Ha!
JEANNIE	Why not? My Granny taught me, you know? I need to keep my hands busy while I'm on breaks at work.
ROXANNE	It's pretty bad, eh?
JEANNIE	It's different. Without your Dad. I've kinda got the lay of the land, there, you know?
ROXANNE	What about Harry?
JEANNIE	Harry is . . . well, he's being patient with me. And the bar is good exercise. Keeps me from going antsy. And it's a social life. Seeing as I'm not playing cards anymore.
ROXANNE	Or screaming at cows.
JEANNIE	Yeah. I think I'll take up knitting. What about you?
ROXANNE	I don't know.
JEANNIE	What do you like doing best?
ROXANNE	Driving. Driving fast.
JEANNIE	Yeah. Like the way they drive ambulances.
ROXANNE	Yeah. Like that.

JEANNIE	Hope I never wind up in one of those things. I'll be content to lie right here, where I came from, when it's time.
ROXANNE	You'd have to learn a lot of first aid stuff for that job. And there's all that special equipment.
JEANNIE	You could do it. Look how you busted your ass to pass.
ROXANNE	Yeah.
JEANNIE	You can go anywhere now.
ROXANNE	Yeah, I know.
JEANNIE	Sorry about Grad.
ROXANNE	I'm glad I didn't buy a dress. Would have just worn it once, anyway.
JEANNIE	You really got gypped.
ROXANNE	Not really.
JEANNIE	What about the coat I never made you?
ROXANNE	There's that.
JEANNIE	And your Dad down at Harry's all the time.
ROXANNE	And you going haywire.
JEANNIE	(*Pause*) Why didn't you go?
ROXANNE	Why didn't you?
JEANNIE	This is better.
ROXANNE	Yeah. (*Pause*) Hey, I got you something. It was in Grade 12. Oh, I hope I didn't burn it! Ah! Here it is. For you. From me.

Roxanne pulls out the envelope with her Grad photo. Jeannie holds it close to the fire to see.

JEANNIE	This is something to keep, all right. You look so grown up in that gown. And they give you roses to hold.
ROXANNE	Fake, Mom.
JEANNIE	Well, we got our corsages, and these are real, eh, even though we didn't go to the dinner dance.

Cowboy Boots and a Corsage, FemFest: Andrea Dziadek as Roxanne and Cairn Moore as Jeannie. Photo by Lynn Kohler.

ROXANNE	Yeah.
JEANNIE	And you got your Grade 12. It's yours forever. Can't get stolen, or burnt down or sold, or beat up. Like Granny used to say, no one can take away what you put in your head.
ROXANNE	Just like your land. Tough grass.
JEANNIE	Like you.
ROXANNE	What about the old homestead up there? It's still standing.
JEANNIE	Falling apart. When I was your age, I used to think about coming out here and fixing it up.
ROXANNE	With Dad?
JEANNIE	Yeah. The night we made you we were out here. I can tell by the moon. It was this time of year, about this time of night.
ROXANNE	Right here?
JEANNIE	The night before we took off for the hills.
ROXANNE	Wow.
JEANNIE	That was a landmark for me. Making you.
ROXANNE	Here.
JEANNIE	I was wearing my cowboy boots.
ROXANNE	You've got boots?
JEANNIE	I used to. I wonder what happened to them.
ROXANNE	They're probably downstairs somewhere. You keep everything.
JEANNIE	Could use them at work.
ROXANNE	I could get them into shape for you.
JEANNIE	I'd like that.
ROXANNE	You could probably still fix up the old place.
JEANNIE	It's good to have it to think about. But I doubt I'll ever do it.
ROXANNE	Yeah. Too busy knitting.

Music. Fade to black.

The Early Worm Club,
Jagged Edge Theatre:
Ian Horobin as Randy,
Christopher Menu
as Jarret and Hansi
Klemm as Millie.
Photo by Ian Jackson.

The EARLY WORM CLUB

The Early Worm Club was first produced by Jagged Edge Lunchbox Theatre, in Edmonton, Alberta, from 30 March to 22 April 2000, with the following cast and crew:

MILLIE Hansi Klemm
RANDY Ian Horobin
JARRET Christopher Menu

DIRECTOR Lisa Newman
STAGE MANAGER Amy DeFelice
PRODUCTION Lisa Newman
SET DESIGN Trevor Schmidt
LIGHT DESIGN Roy Jackson
SOUND DESIGN Katherine Koller, Amy DeFelice, and Christopher Menu

Characters

MILLIE, thirties, unattached, recent devotee of bird watching, completely
  adorned in the paraphernalia of her new "therapy"

RANDY, late twenties, a bachelor, holds a steady job, plays outfielder on the
  baseball team, a lifelong urbanite

JARRET, thirties, divorced, pitcher on Randy's recreational baseball team for
  the last few years, with a wolflike familiarity of the woods. Randy sometimes
  calls him "Jar," pronounced "Jer."

Time
The present. Early summer.

Place
Wooded parkland

Set
A suggestion of trees, with places for being seen and unseen in various levels
of the trees, is necessary. Lighting defines the passage from night to dawn to
morning.

Music
Vocals, unaccompanied, or minimally accompanied, such as Gregorian chant,
scat singing, or spirituals. A separate musical selection can be used as a motif
for each of the three characters to introduce their monologues.

SCENE 1 Very early Saturday morning

Music. Jarret and Randy enter. Randy is carrying a heavy knapsack.

RANDY   I should be in bed.

JARRET   When you're alone, bed ain't gonna work.

RANDY   So what is this gonna do?

JARRET   Breathe deep.

RANDY   All I need is sleep.

JARRET   That comes later.

RANDY   It's almost day.

JARRET   First I've got to clear my head.

RANDY   But I need to go to the laundromat.

JARRET   Big plans.

RANDY   I might meet the girl of my dreams at the laundromat.

JARRET   Give it up. They're all flakes.

RANDY   I don't think so. What about that girl, Lesley, at the party?

JARRET   She was okay.

RANDY   See?

JARRET   Marry her and she'd turn into a flake.

Randy stops to put sack down, opens it and looks inside.

RANDY   What is in here?

JARRET   I'll take it. Keep moving. Gotta keep the blood circulating.

RANDY   Evaporate the alcohol.

JARRET   Next weekend, it's your turn to get plastered.

RANDY   I can hardly wait. Lesley would love me. Spewing out
               of the car, honking the horn.

The Early Worm Club   41

JARRET	So maybe I should be a monk. They have monks who make jam, so why not monks who do drywall? You put your stilts on, no talking, look up and do the ceiling over and over again like Michelangelo. And you never go through married hell.
RANDY	Three years of marriage and one divorce and you want to be a monk. You're way ahead of me.

Randy sits, blending into the trees.

JARRET	Miles.

Jarret keeps walking, downstage.

JARRET	The guy is like plaster dust, eh? Always checking on me, making me eat stuff at the party. I tell him, for me, drinking is, like, a ritual, eh? I don't eat before, during or after. Too hard on the gut, eh? I take my booze in pure form. (*Pause*) Everybody thinks I'm out for chicks, eh? Nope, I'm a monk. There's only one woman for me, and she dumped me on my ass. Probably got ten new guys who want her now. She turns heads. Body like a sculpture. Smart, too. Got her own job. Personnel manager. She wants kids. I can't stand to sit beside 'em.

Jarret moves into the tree. Millie enters, resets her binoculars, hat, book, pen.

MILLIE	What I'm looking for is any sign of movement, any hope of life. A tiny alteration in the scenery. If I don't see anything, then I . . . listen. They're up there, hiding in the canopy. (*Pause*) Wouldn't you love to be with them, away from all the dirt of life, gradually covering you up, sinking you deeper into the ground? Up there, the air must be so pure, totally oxygenated from all those leaves? Hey? I'd have a snug little nest. I would fly! Oh, and if you're a bird your genes come with an annual built-in winter vacation! I'd like the camaraderie, the flocking, you know?

Millie gets down, takes off her paraphernalia, lies down as if asleep, then pretends to wake up like Snow White.

Do you remember when Snow White is left in the woods by the kind-hearted huntsman and she's in a clearing, and all the animals of the forest come out? They all want to be her friend? I'd sit out here forever if there was a chance they'd show themselves for me — you know, the birds and all the little creatures?

Millie gets up.

If I don't see or hear a bird for a day or two, I get really anxious. I think the world is coming to an end. To me, every bird is a miracle. I grew up on a farm, and we had this old rooster who crowed like the dickens. Cock-a-doodle-doo! We called him His Lordship. When I was little, I thought it was the voice of God.

Sound of owl hooting.

One lonely screech of the owl: "One for sorrow, two for mirth, three for a wedding, and four for a birth." Huh, sorrow.

Millie resets her gear.

But, when I set off to go in the woods to watch birds, I feel very safe. The time I'm out here is a safety factor. Nobody's up at five for a stroll in the woods, except a fellow birdwatcher or maybe a friendly huntsman.

Jarret hides in the trees, taking out a softball from the bag and throwing it at Randy.

RANDY   Hey!

JARRET   Just testing your night vision.

RANDY   How long do you want to stay here?

JARRET   Until we see something.

RANDY   What are we looking for?

JARRET   Birds.

RANDY	Sure.
JARRET	Yeah. Listen.
RANDY	Listen for what?
JARRET	Birds.
RANDY	Yeah, right.
JARRET	(*Tossing binoculars*) See what you see.
RANDY	A couple of guys wandering the woods in the dark.
JARRET	What was that?
RANDY	What?
JARRET	I heard something.
RANDY	Something big?
JARRET	Maybe.
RANDY	Like a bear?
JARRET	(*Laughs*) You scared of bears?
RANDY	(*Climbing*) What is it?
JARRET	A deer. You scared it off.
RANDY	I think I'll stay up here.
JARRET	You'll scare off all the birds.
RANDY	So what.
JARRET	I gotta see some birds before we go.
RANDY	You saw a deer.
JARRET	It's gotta be birds.
RANDY	Why?
JARRET	Because birds make me feel better!
RANDY	(*Coming down*) If you ask me, we're looking for the wrong kind of birds.

Millie is unseen by Randy or Jarret.

MILLIE	It's really amazing how many birds you've already seen, like in your past, before you took up the sport? See, here in the index of this book, I outline the little box for each species in green if I remember seeing it before, like if I recognize it from the photograph but I never knew its name? The author of this book says you don't really know a bird until you know its Latin name, but I'm sticking with the, well, vulgar names. I don't know why they say vulgar. I mean, do we say avifauna or do we say birds? Anyway, once I've seen a bird and know its name, I colour the square in red. Look at this page. Five red boxes already.
JARRET	There's a redpoll at four o' clock.

Millie checks her book.

RANDY	Oh? Okay. That's it, then. We can go, right?
JARRET	Wait a minute. There's a finch.
RANDY	Hallelujah.
JARRET	Little, bright yellow. Over there.
RANDY	(*Sees Millie*) Oh.
JARRET	And a flicker flying by. I can hear a woodpecker, can you?
RANDY	Hi.
MILLIE	Shh.
JARRET	There's a swallow, and a cowbird, and I think that was a female redwing blackbird.
MILLIE	Wow. He's good.
RANDY	I guess.
JARRET	Osprey way up there, heading toward the water.
MILLIE	(*To Jarret*) I hear the male redwing.
JARRET	What the . . . ? Who is she?
RANDY	I don't know. She's been watching you.

MILLIE	Hear it? There. I knew there would be a pair. I'm Millie.
JARRET	What are you doing in my space?
MILLIE	I'm . . . looking for birds. Just like you.
JARRET	Yeah? Well, you can do it over there. We were here first.
MILLIE	You can't do that. Birders are friendly folks.
JARRET	You're interrupting me.
MILLIE	Is he serious or what?
RANDY	Jarret? Oh, he's just hungover.
MILLIE	Talk about clouding you over before it's even morning yet.
RANDY	Yeah. Sorry. He's a pretty crusty guy. He does drywall.
MILLIE	Oh.
RANDY	I'm Randy. I'm an accountant.
MILLIE	Oh, you're probably one of those listers.
RANDY	Listers?
MILLIE	Yeah. How long is yours?
RANDY	I . . . I'm not sure!
JARRET	Would you butt out?
MILLIE	Sorry. Shhh.

Silence.

JARRET	I was on a real roll there.
MILLIE	I . . . I . . .
JARRET	Don't talk.

Silence.

RANDY	Maybe we should go.
JARRET	I didn't get my quota. I need to get my quota.
RANDY	What's that?

JARRET	Ten birds. I only got eight.
MILLIE	A quota counter.
JARRET	Don't talk.

Silence.

RANDY	There's one.
JARRET	Where?
RANDY	Sitting on that branch at two o'clock.
JARRET	What is that?
MILLIE	It's a robin.
JARRET	A basic robin.
MILLIE	Yes.
RANDY	Yeah, it does look like a robin!
JARRET	That's only nine.
MILLIE	One more and I can move.
JARRET	Don't talk.

Silence. Rain.

MILLIE	(*Unpacking umbrella, rain gear*) I knew it.
JARRET	What?
MILLIE	It's raining. That little lull in the birdsong? That happens a lot out here just before it starts to sprinkle.
JARRET	Do you ever stop?
MILLIE	Did you know that was a secret of the monks? They had the stamina of athletes. They'd only sleep a few hours a day, but they kept their energy up by singing almost all their waking hours. The chants gave them the power to function with very little rest.
RANDY	Like birds.

MILLIE	In the bird kingdom, the male who starts singing nonstop during the early morning feeding hours is considered the strongest, the most virile, for being able to perform without any food.
JARRET	Makes sense.

Silence.

RANDY	Uh, it's really raining. Maybe I should go get the car.
JARRET	Good idea.
RANDY	(*To Millie*) Would you like a ride to your car?
MILLIE	I took a bus and hiked in.
RANDY	Can we drive you back to the city?
MILLIE	Thanks, I think I'll stay.
JARRET	Go get the car.
RANDY	Okay. Uh, just over there?
JARRET	It's the only car in the parking lot.

Randy moves downstage.

RANDY	Yeah, well, I've never been good with girls. Because I don't have my own, I've sorta made one up in my mind. She talks to me, tells me she'll be around soon, to keep looking out for her . . . stuff like my mother would say, you know?

Pause.

The guys bug me. They see my tattoo, it says "Mandy," and they think I'm just as experienced as they are. I had a dog once called Mandy.

Pause.

My lady. I'm not so scared of the woods and the rain when I tell myself she's waiting for me.

Randy exits.

MILLIE	So Randy tells me you're a drywaller.
JARRET	Yeah. I make walls. Miles and miles of white, smooth walls. Lotsa dust. Lotsa sweat. Sweat 'n dust walls.
MILLIE	I don't like walls.
JARRET	Corners. Those are the worst. I hate corners. I'm in these rooms, newly finished walls, and I think, there's no space in here. I'm going to suffocate.
MILLIE	Do you think about here?
JARRET	Yeah. I go out and party but I always end up here.
MILLIE	And let the morning light lift you with it.
JARRET	Yeah.
MILLIE	I'm surprised I haven't seen you out here before.
JARRET	Most days, I've got my ten birds right away and I'm gone.
MILLIE	Have you ever heard of the caladrius?
JARRET	Sounds Latin or something.
MILLIE	I think so.
JARRET	I don't like Latin.
MILLIE	Neither do I. But anyway, the caladrius was an ancient mythical bird thought to be able to absorb the illness of the man who gazed on it and then fly the sickness to the heavens where it couldn't do any harm.
JARRET	Sounds like monk talk.
MILLIE	I just wondered if your fixation with seeing birds is a carryover from a very old way of healing.
JARRET	I don't know! I might as well be a monk, eh, if you count how long I've been . . . what's that word?
MILLIE	Celibate?
JARRET	Yeah.

MILLIE	That's a Latin word.
JARRET	That's for sure.
MILLIE	Rain's stopping.

Silence. Millie moves closer.

JARRET	Good. I want to see my number ten.
MILLIE	Oh.

Silence.

JARRET	In my job, you mess up when you talk. You make bumps. The smoothest walls come from the quietest guys.
MILLIE	You must be good at . . . what you do.
JARRET	Smooth it over, smooth it over. Yeah, work and baseball.
MILLIE	And birding.
JARRET	Not bad.
MILLIE	(*Unhappily*) There's a crow.
JARRET	I don't count crows.
MILLIE	(*Brightening*) Oh? Some people think they are lucky.
JARRET	I shoot them and cook them.
MILLIE	You eat crows?
JARRET	Only on Hallowe'en.

Silence.

MILLIE	I'm not fond of cormorants myself. Sea crows. They remind me of witches, you know, when they lift their wings to dry them? They look like they're going to pounce on you.

Jarret poses as a cormorant.

MILLIE	Do you want a sandwich?
JARRET	(*Lifting the top slice of bread*) No.
MILLIE	Oh.

Silence.

MILLIE	Randy is taking his time.
JARRET	Probably lost.
MILLIE	The light's coming.
JARRET	He'd need someone holding his hand to get out of these woods.
MILLIE	So why didn't you go with him?
JARRET	I'm waiting for my ten. Doesn't anybody get that?

Silence.

JARRET	Where are they? They should be coming out to feed.
MILLIE	How's your head?
JARRET	It was about nine-tenths gone, but now it's starting to buzz.
MILLIE	Maybe something to eat?
JARRET	I told you, NO.
MILLIE	I wonder why people say "eat like a bird"? Birds eat a lot. All that energy bringing up their babies and then a major migration right after? They eat like pigs, actually. All the time. And "bird-brained"? I don't know why they say that, because birds must be the smartest creatures in the world to fly halfway around it every year and find their old homes. (*Pause*) Why do you like birds, Jarret?
JARRET	I like their singing.
MILLIE	The sound bath.
JARRET	I guess.

MILLIE	The auditorium of the air.
JARRET	Best there is.
MILLIE	No walls.
JARRET	No echo.
MILLIE	Sanctuary.
JARRET	Escape.

Sound of oriole.

MILLIE	What's that?
JARRET	An oriole. It's gonna be up high. They hardly ever come down.

Randy enters. Birdsong stops.

RANDY	Hey, did you guys see that orange thing up there?
JARRET	Where?
RANDY	Well, it's gone now but it was right over your heads.
JARRET	Thanks, pal!
RANDY	I waited 'til it went, Jar.
JARRET	I'm going to look for it.
MILLIE	I'll come, too.
JARRET	No. You stay put. I need some space.
RANDY	I've got the car running on the road. I thought you guys might be soaked and frozen.
MILLIE	You're the one who's soaked and frozen. Hot tea?
RANDY	Oh, yeah.

Jarret moves to his own space.

JARRET	I can't breathe with that guy around. And then her! I need quiet, eh?

Pause.

> The only sound I can take is these birds. It doesn't poke at my brain, you know? It, like, glues me back together. Smoothes me out.

Pause.

> That oriole may have screwed me up. And this rain. I don't like orioles. Well, so they sing okay. But they're show-offs, eh? They don't let you see 'em. They just, like, tantalize you. Hear me, but, whoops! Don't see me. And then Randy goes and sees 'em. What does he know?

Jarret exits.

MILLIE	How about a sandwich?
RANDY	Oh, fantastic. I'm starving. (*Bites*) Um, this is good. Crunchy. Lots of veggies. All veggies.
MILLIE	You get hungrier out here.
RANDY	Yeah. So. Are you ready to go?
MILLIE	I don't think so. The sun's trying to come up, it's going to stop raining. I think I'll stay. Thanks anyway.
RANDY	Well, in that case, I'll wait 'til Jarret gets back. If it's okay with you.
MILLIE	You don't care about your car out there, running, polluting the lungs of the birds?
RANDY	My car? It hardly breathes when it's running. I use clean gas.
MILLIE	I used to have a car. I used to be a chain smoker. It went with the job. Advertising.
RANDY	So how did you quit?
MILLIE	One day the boss gave me the cash to go meet his supplier of, uh, recreational cigarettes. So I left with the money, which is about what he owed me, and never went back.

RANDY	Then I got on as a mail carrier, but when all you do is look up at the trees, you don't watch the addresses on all your pieces, and you mess up. So then I decided on birdwatching, and I made up the Early Worm Club.
RANDY	Who's in it?
MILLIE	Just me. I don't advertise. I could, at the Nature Centre where I work now. But I don't. Next Saturday is my anniversary meeting.

Car horn honking.

MILLIE	That must be Jarret.
RANDY	Why the Early Worm Club?
MILLIE	Well, the worms are out before the birds are.
RANDY	Surely you don't see yourself as a . . . worm.
MILLIE	Oh, yes. We all are, us poor earthlings. The birds are privy to the heavens while we twist in the dirt.
RANDY	Um. You're sure you don't want a ride?
MILLIE	Uh huh.
RANDY	Well, maybe, could I get your phone number so I could call you tonight and make sure you got home all right?
MILLIE	I'll be fine. Really.
RANDY	I don't feel right about leaving you here like this. But you do this all the time?
MILLIE	Every Saturday rain or shine. Never had a problem I couldn't handle.
RANDY	Bye, then. Uh. Thanks for the sandwich.

Randy exits. Millie climbs up a tree.

MILLIE	Oh, there it is! The rainbow! Oh! Red, orange, yellow, green, blue, indigo, violet! Each colour of the spectrum causes a different physiological response, so you need light from all seven to stay balanced and healthy. So

when you say, "I need some fresh air," you really mean, "I need some full-spectrum light." They've studied it — you're more cooperative when you're outside and you even get fewer cavities!

Pause.

I eat the rainbow, too. I build each meal with something of every colour. Then I'm sure to get all my nutrients. Oh, but not like a blue milkshake or even orange cheese. Chemicals in your food erode your intelligence! I only use natural colours, so I'm visually, psychologically, and physically satisfied.

Pause.

Even with all my colours, though, I think I'm missing something. My body wants . . . a mate. It's ready and waiting. Trimmed and tuned. Regular, uh, happenings, with a loving partner is all I lack, really.

Randy enters.

RANDY	Millie! Millie?
MILLIE	Up here!
RANDY	(*Quickly climbing*) Is there a bear?
MILLIE	No, I just like it up here.
RANDY	Oh.
MILLIE	What do you want?
RANDY	(*Very uncomfortable in tree*) He took my car! He just took off on me. I could see the tail lights spinning around the bend when I got to the road!
MILLIE	But it's your car.
RANDY	Right. So I waited. I thought it was just a trick, a little scare tactic.
MILLIE	Would he do that?

RANDY	Yeah, laughing all the way. I guess I took too long getting there.
MILLIE	Because of me.
RANDY	Oh, don't say that! My only consolation is that I get to hear you talk some more, if that's all right.
MILLIE	I'm planning on doing some serious birdwatching now.
RANDY	Can I watch you watch?
MILLIE	It's up to you. Are you sure he won't come back?
RANDY	We've got a baseball game this afternoon. I guess he figures I'm pretty dispensable.
MILLIE	What do you play?
RANDY	Outfielder.
MILLIE	What about Jarret?
RANDY	He's the pitcher.
MILLIE	Oh.
RANDY	He's probably what you call an attractive guy, right?
MILLIE	Oh, I don't know.
RANDY	All those muscles, the sure-footedness, the commanding manner.
MILLIE	He seems to know his way around the woods.
RANDY	He'd eat you up.
MILLIE	He wasn't hungry.
RANDY	Maybe this time. Next time, who knows?
MILLIE	You put up with him.
RANDY	Yeah. He needs a friend.
MILLIE	Everybody's entitled to a friend.
RANDY	What about you?
MILLIE	Well, the birds are my friends. And then there's Karla.

RANDY	Who's Karla?
MILLIE	She's this girl I work with. She does me a big favour every day, in return for Sunday dinner at my place. She's rather large, and I've got this diet I invented . . . anyway, I don't drive any more.
RANDY	Air pollution.
MILLIE	Yes. So I canoe down the river to work.
RANDY	You're kidding.
MILLIE	No. It's not far, maybe three kilometres. And Karla, you see, meets me at the docking area, helps me strap the canoe on her car, and takes my bike out of her trunk so I can bike home after work.
RANDY	And she helps you launch the canoe in the morning.
MILLIE	Uh huh.
RANDY	Dedicated.
MILLIE	Or something. She's been acting bossy lately, like proposing Sunday night sleepovers and hinting about moving in with me.
RANDY	Oh-oh.
MILLIE	The thing is, I couldn't canoe May to November without her. Fall is my favourite. The colours are so beautiful they make me stop and cry. (*Pause*) Oh, this feels so reckless, but I wonder if you . . . and Jarret . . . would come to my anniversary meeting next Saturday? The club will be a year old, and maybe it's time to ask some other people to . . .
RANDY	I'll come for sure. I'll ask Jarret.
MILLIE	I wonder if he found his number ten.
RANDY	No doubt. A turkey.
MILLIE	You really put yourself down a lot. You should watch that.
RANDY	I can't even hold on to my own wheels.

MILLIE	That's Jarret exerting his power over you.
RANDY	I'd like to punch him.
MILLIE	You look like the kind of guy who has a good job, takes care of his own laundry, gets fed by relatives regularly, gets along with his relatives, has a few hobbies, but . . .
RANDY	But what?
MILLIE	You're not obsessive about anything.
RANDY	I have my plans, hopes, I have my dreams.
MILLIE	You're probably going to build a house someday, have a family, be normal.
RANDY	Yeah, so what's wrong with that?
MILLIE	You don't really stand out.
RANDY	Okay. I can take this. I'm not remarkable. I need an obsession to make me interesting?
MILLIE	Well, yeah.
RANDY	I thought women liked steadiness, surety, dependability.
MILLIE	It's too predictable.
RANDY	I was wrong about you, then.
MILLIE	What?
RANDY	I think you have a terrific voice. I thought I'd heard you before, in my dreams.
MILLIE	Sure.
RANDY	My lady. I know I'll find her in a really strange place . . .
MILLIE	See? Out of the ordinary. Not like the laundromat or something boring. You're looking for new, strange, obsessive.
RANDY	I guess I am.
MILLIE	Don't worry. You will find her. You will be happy ever after.

RANDY	I hope so, because right now it's guys like Jarret who have all the fun. Jarret goes from girl to girl, never satisfied.
MILLIE	He does?
RANDY	He doesn't want anything new. He wants his girl to stay the same.
MILLIE	Why?
RANDY	He can't stand change. Or any sign of aging, maturing. He'd do better with a statue.
MILLIE	That would be a waste.
RANDY	If I found her, this lady I listen to in my dreams, I'd take her home with me no matter what. She could be deformed and I would still want her. Forever.
MILLIE	Randy! That's better.
RANDY	You like that.
MILLIE	Yeah. That is . . . very attractive.

Jarret enters, mock shooting at Millie and Randy.

JARRET	Two of a kind.
MILLIE	Oh, Jarret! (*Climbing down*)
RANDY	Hey! (*Climbing down*)
JARRET	We've got a game in an hour!
RANDY	I thought you took off!
JARRET	I only went around the block. I hate sitting still when the motor's running.
RANDY	Must have been a big block.
JARRET	C'mon. You said you had to hit the laundromat.
RANDY	I can skip it.
JARRET	But you always go to the laundromat.
RANDY	Not today!

MILLIE	Jarret! What was your ten?
JARRET	A couple of grouse in a tree, just waiting to be popped off.
MILLIE	This is parkland!
JARRET	So what? (*To Randy*) Are you ready?
RANDY	When you hand over my keys.
MILLIE	Wait! Jarret, I just want to know, how did you get to be such a good birder?
JARRET	Robbing nests and hunting.
RANDY	Keys?

Jarret passes keys.

MILLIE	(*To Jarret*) Good luck at the game!
RANDY	Thanks. See you next Saturday.
MILLIE	You, too, Jarret.
JARRET	Uh, let's go. They can't start without us.

Randy and Jarret exit.
Millie climbs down, finds Jarret's knapsack.

MILLIE	Oh. Treasures. Oh. (*Takes Jarret's baseball glove, smells it, loves it, tries it on*) This is nice. Smooth leather. Big hand. Oh, yeah. Keep this. My huntsman. My hunt. (*Puts it in her own pack*) Finders keepers, okay? Normally I wouldn't ever have anything made of leather. I'm very anti-leather, anti-fur, anti-meat. This may be a problem with Jarret. He's obviously a meat-eater, the way he inspected my sprout and tomato sandwich. But I changed and so can he. What going vegetarian did for my PMS will do for his drinking. Jarret's got a good eye, even with the effects of all that alcohol. He'd be stunning after a purifying rainbow diet.

Jarret enters, calling off to Randy, who follows soon after.

JARRET	I'll get it! Go back to the car.
MILLIE	I bet you need this.
JARRET	(*To Randy*) I've got it! Let's go! (*Checks knapsack*)
RANDY	Oh, good. Thanks, Millie. We thought you may have taken it home for us or something.
JARRET	Wait a sec. The mitt's gone. Where's the mitt?
RANDY	It was in there. I saw it.
JARRET	It's gone.
MILLIE	Well, let's look around. Now, did the knapsack go up the tree with you, Randy?
RANDY	No. You had it, Jar. You tossed me the ball, I tossed it back and you stuck it in the bag. Maybe it fell out somewhere.
JARRET	Start looking.
MILLIE	It's got to be here somewhere.
RANDY	Geez, Jar, we've only got a half hour to get there. And we need to pick up some food.
MILLIE	(*Opening her knapsack, but hiding glove*) I've got some lunch here if you want to take it with you.
RANDY	Well that's . . .
JARRET	No way. We'll get burgers. Athlete food.
RANDY	Well, I don't see your glove.
MILLIE	Hey, guys, how about I stay around and look for it. It's got to be here, somewhere, and then next Saturday I'll meet you, like I was telling Randy, and I'll give it to you then. Okay, Jarret?
JARRET	Aw! I need my glove.
RANDY	You can borrow someone's.
JARRET	I hate that. Ugh.
RANDY	We've got to go.

JARRET	Okay. Because this is an emergency, here's my phone number. (*Hands card*) If you find it, you call me.
MILLIE	Will do. Good luck.
RANDY	Bye, Millie.
JARRET	This is going to screw the game for me. Geez, and I got my ten. I always play great when I see ten.

Randy and Jarret exit.

MILLIE	Oh, yes!

Millie memorizes the phone number and tucks the card into her sock.
Music. Dance dream interlude. Millie pretends to use the glove, while Randy and Jarret warm up for the game. Jarret is bare-handed; Randy has a glove. They play while Millie tries, "pig in the middle," unsuccessfully, to intercept the ball. She's just not in the same time or place. Randy misses a ball and Millie runs offstage to find it.
Randy and Jarret continue playing as if they haven't lost a ball, using another from Jarret's pocket. They gradually move offstage.

SCENE 2 Next Saturday morning

Millie enters with knapsack and a large picnic basket.

MILLIE	I called him six times. Once per day. Different times of the day. I left six messages, all with my phone number repeated twice. I've hardly had a night's sleep the whole week, waiting for him to call back; that was not smart, I know. And apart from going to work, I didn't go out at all. So, by today, I feel quite deprived of rainbow light.

Pause. Millie reveals an egg, which she peels.

I had quite a time deciding what to pack for lunch. I settled on egg. . . . I know what you're thinking about the mayonnaise, but I've got a little cooler in here, runs on a battery? Eggs are also a bird thing, if you know what I mean. I was trying to keep to a theme. Also, did you know that ancient tribes believed you could enhance your own qualities by eating the part of the bird that corresponded? Well, I picked eggs because, you know, they're for attraction, mating, fertility?

Pause.

Even though he didn't return my calls, I think he'll come. He wants his glove back. I can tell he's superstitious about it. I've slept with it every night. I tucked it in, put my arm around it, and breathed in his aroma. During the day, I stuffed the inside of the glove with a pair of socks, hoping they would absorb the smell, so I'd have something that smells like him to sleep with tonight.

Randy enters, with picnic basket and a baseball bat.

RANDY	Millie!
MILLIE	Hi!
RANDY	I was just on my way to a game.
MILLIE	Is Jarret with you?
RANDY	No. I told him about it last Saturday, but he had an out-of-town job this week so I haven't talked to him since.
MILLIE	Oh.
RANDY	I brought a . . . oh, you brought one, too.
MILLIE	Well, let's hope Jarret comes so we can eat up all this food later. There's enough for your whole baseball team!
RANDY	So how have you been?
MILLIE	Fine. You?
RANDY	I've been looking forward to coming out here all week.
MILLIE	How did the game go?
RANDY	Considering I didn't get any sleep the night before, I had a great game. I had three hits and got one guy out.

MILLIE	Wow. How did Jarret do?
RANDY	He was a mess without his glove. I've never seen him so whacked.
MILLIE	Too bad.
RANDY	He's got this thing about that glove. His ex gave it to him.
MILLIE	Oh.
RANDY	So, see anything yet today?
MILLIE	Oh, no. I just got here.
RANDY	I saw that old orange bird again, caught just a glimpse of it.
MILLIE	The oriole? I hope it comes back. Jarret would like to see it, too.
RANDY	Jarret is . . . a wolf.
MILLIE	Well, I'm not Little Red Riding Hood.
RANDY	I didn't mean that you were.
MILLIE	I never believed that story, you know. I mean, if a wolf is hungry, he'll eat you, but he's not going to dress up like your grandmother to do it.
RANDY	I love how you are so independent. Like with your club. Tell me some more about it.
MILLIE	Well. Okay. This is its first anniversary. I started it last year on my birth —
RANDY	It's your birthday?
MILLIE	Yes. And I thought this one would be really special.
RANDY	I get to be the first one to wish you happy birthday.
MILLIE	You're probably the only one.
RANDY	Well, it's better than nobody, isn't it? After all, you did invite me.
MILLIE	I did. And I could count on you to be punctual and thoughtful enough to bring a picnic.

RANDY	We can stay out all day. We can have mine for lunch and yours for supper, if you want.
MILLIE	What about the game?
RANDY	Well, a picnic is portable. We could have it at the park after the game.
MILLIE	I'd like to go to the game.
RANDY	Then it's a date.
MILLIE	Okay.
RANDY	I visited the Nature Centre this week. I didn't see you there.
MILLIE	Oh?
RANDY	I met Karla. She told me it was your day off. I thought Saturday was your day off.
MILLIE	I work a four-day week. It's much healthier. I went to the laundromat on my day off.
RANDY	Oh?
MILLIE	I thought maybe you guys didn't get a chance last Saturday.
RANDY	How did you know which laundromat?
MILLIE	I picked the one closest to where Jarret lives.
RANDY	I do mine at Snow White Laundry.
MILLIE	You do?
RANDY	Yeah.
MILLIE	That's in my neighbourhood!
RANDY	Really? I've never seen you there!
MILLIE	I've never seen you there. But if you go on Saturdays, we'd miss each other because I'm always out here on Saturdays.
RANDY	I think it would be lonely out here all by yourself.

MILLIE	Here I feel bound to all of life. When you saw that bird this morning, didn't it give you a lift?
RANDY	Well, yes. I wanted to tell you about it.
MILLIE	But it's a gift that you saw it. You wouldn't see it in the city.
RANDY	But I've seen birds in the city. Lots of them are fed by feeders.
MILLIE	Yeah, and lots are killed by flying into buildings in the downtown core. I'm on the board for FLAP, Fatal Light Awareness Program. Twice a week I go downtown before dawn and cover up shocked birds, wait with them until they resuscitate, feed them water and fend off the cats.
RANDY	Wow. I like the birds you see in flocks in the middle of winter.
MILLIE	On the coldest January day, when you think there can't be a living thing breathing outside, a swirl of cedar waxwings appears to remind you of the power of life.
RANDY	Yeah, and I've always liked going out to the lake. I get the same feeling out there.
MILLIE	What do you like about the lake?
RANDY	The quiet, really. All you get is the sound of the bonfire when the others have gone off to bed.
MILLIE	I bet you keep the fire burning, Randy.
RANDY	Yeah, I do. Then I like taking off all my clothes and going swimming, when the water feels so warm, and I like looking at the stars.
MILLIE	I'd like to go owling sometime, and witness the secrets of the dark.
RANDY	If you've spent all your nights in the city, then you've missed the stars. You can't see them like you can out here.
MILLIE	Light pollution. I know.

RANDY	I have another place I like. You'd like it, too. My mother's garden. I go over most Sundays to help her with the heavy work. When I'm in that place, I swear all my muscles relax. I smell all those fresh smells and I eat this big dinner . . .
MILLIE	Are you hungry?
RANDY	Yeah, I could eat now.
MILLIE	Red wine?
RANDY	I brought white.
MILLIE	I like both.
RANDY	So do I.

Jarret enters.

JARRET	Aw, isn't this cozy?
MILLIE	We were just starting.
JARRET	I'm not staying. I just want my glove.
MILLIE	Some wine?
JARRET	I want my mitt.
MILLIE	Spring water?
JARRET	Give me my glove, woman.
MILLIE	Are you sure? An egg sandwich?
JARRET	I'm so sure.
MILLIE	Did you get my messages?
JARRET	Oh, yeah. Day and night, all week. What a pain.
MILLIE	I just wanted to let you know your glove was safe.
JARRET	One night was in the middle of Taffy and me . . .
RANDY	Taffy is the ex-wife.
MILLIE	Oh.
JARRET	Not for long. She's coming around. She's coming to the game today and I'm going to be wonderful. That's why I'm not drinking. And that's why I want the glove. Now!

RANDY	You don't have to be rude.
MILLIE	It's right here.
JARRET	And I know you had it all along. It wasn't lost at all, was it?
MILLIE	I just wanted to see you again.
JARRET	Well, you've seen me, and I'm not available. Taffy's back in town. This time I'm going to do everything right.
MILLIE	I'll be cheering for you.
JARRET	What?
RANDY	Millie's coming to the game. My date.
JARRET	Just don't talk to me. Don't even come near me. Taffy is a very jealous woman.
MILLIE	Oh.
JARRET	And she is the only woman for me.
RANDY	Hope you patch it up with her, Jarret.
JARRET	This time for sure. Ugh. What is this smell on my glove?
MILLIE	What smell?
JARRET	Like bath oil or something.
MILLIE	Oh, it may have absorbed the scent of my . . . potpourri.
JARRET	Doesn't smell like my mitt anymore!
MILLIE	Oh, it does. Leathery and lean.
JARRET	How do you know? Have you been sleeping with it or something?
RANDY	Jarret, get real.
JARRET	Taffy's got a nose for stuff like this. She'll go berserk.
MILLIE	She sniffs your things?
JARRET	What am I going to do?
RANDY	Let's warm it up. Here.

Randy and Jarret play catch.

MILLIE	You've got a great arm, Jarret.
JARRET	You can't say stuff like that in front of Taffy, I'm warning you.
MILLIE	I think I know what you mean. I have this friend, Karla.
RANDY	Yeah, she nearly decapitated me when I asked for you at the Nature Centre.
MILLIE	Thing is, it makes me like her less.
JARRET	Makes me crazy about Taf.
MILLIE	Oh. Have you got it good and sweaty yet?
JARRET	What?
MILLIE	The glove. Let me smell it. Oh, yeah. That's a baseball glove smell.
JARRET	When I smell this glove . . . I smell you! You violated my glove! Taffy gave me this glove! She'll go nuts if she finds out. Stay away!

Jarret exits.

RANDY	Are you okay?
MILLIE	I've felt worse. Like the time I had a date and the next day the man sent me a white rose, and I didn't know what it meant until I never heard from him again. He was European. I guess it meant, "This is dead." Then there was this sweet farm boy who told me after our first date, "Well, honey, it's no good beating a dead horse."
RANDY	Some people are just not meant for some people.
MILLIE	Jarret must really love her, hey?
RANDY	I've never seen him turn down a drink before. Maybe Taffy will be good for him this time.
MILLIE	I bet she only eats junk food.
RANDY	I wish we could go back to where we were.

MILLIE	I'm not very hungry anymore.
RANDY	Don't let him wreck our picnic. That's what he wanted to do. Let's not give him the satisfaction.
MILLIE	Somehow I don't think he's really gone. I think he's still in the woods.
RANDY	He's gone. Now, where was I? I was going to have one of your sandwiches.
MILLIE	Randy, did you lock your car?
RANDY	No. Why?
MILLIE	You don't think he would do anything, I mean, to make sure we don't get to the game?
RANDY	I better go check. (*Takes bat*) I'll be right back.

Randy exits.
Millie packs baskets.

MILLIE	I've spent a whole week permeating my environment with the thought of him and now it's going to take a whole week to exterminate him. I'm very strict about my environment. When I take something in, like Jarret's glove, I take something out in exchange, to provide equilibrium and prevent clutter. So I got rid of an old bird cage. From my advertising days. When I brought Jarret's glove home, the cage seemed like the symbolic thing to remove. I felt so free, so released!

Pause.

	I think I imprinted on him. It wasn't fair, really. I mean to say about someone you don't even know, "This is the man for me." But he was in my territory. What if he comes back? No, he won't. Not if I'm here.

Millie takes her basket and climbs the tree as before.
Randy enters.

RANDY	Millie? It's okay! I found him trying to pull the ignition fuse but I scared him off . . . Millie? Millie! Millie.

Randy climbs, more sure-footed than last time.

RANDY Millie. It's all right. I'm here. You're not the only one in your club anymore.

MILLIE I . . . I just have to purge him out. A good cry, a little meditation, a day of fasting . . .

RANDY Fast? Not me. I'm having one of your sandwiches. I've got a game to play later, and a lady watching.

MILLIE I don't know about the game, Randy. I think I'll just go home.

RANDY No way. It's your birthday. I want you to have some fun.

MILLIE I don't want to see Jarret again. I'd rather not go.

RANDY Okay. We won't go. I'll miss the game.

MILLIE You don't seem like the type to miss anything.

RANDY This is an exceptional circumstance. It's Millie's birthday.

Sound of orioles singing.

RANDY The orioles!

MILLIE I hear the male. I see the female.

RANDY It's a sign, Millie. It's got to be.

MILLIE There's the male!

RANDY I don't think they wanted to share themselves with anyone . . .

MILLIE . . . but us!

RANDY Millie, would you come with me to my mother's tomorrow?

MILLIE Sunday?

RANDY You'd have to cancel Karla.

MILLIE I'd like to cancel Karla.

RANDY Millie, I'll carry your canoe.

Sound of two pellet gun shots.

MILLIE	Randy!
RANDY	Get down!

Pause. Jarret enters, throws the birds down.

JARRET	Throw some dirt on 'em. See if they move.
MILLIE	How could you?
JARRET	They never come down where you can see them.
MILLIE	So now they're flat on the dirt like the rest of us.
JARRET	Not me. I'm flyin'.
RANDY	You're sick.
MILLIE	You said you liked their song, but you don't, really. You just like knowing what they all are, like targets.
JARRET	C'mon. Let's get to the game.
RANDY	No.
JARRET	Get a move on. Taffy's waiting in my truck.
RANDY	Find yourself a new outfielder.
JARRET	We're going to win today.
RANDY	Not interested.
JARRET	What a loser. Look at her!

Millie picks the birds up and cradles them in her skirt.

RANDY	(*Shoves bat at Jarret*) You can take your stinking baseball team! I'm not coming back!
JARRET	Some friend.

Sound of truck horn honking.
Jarret takes the bat and exits.

MILLIE	Why did you let him see you? Show yourself to the wolf and you're dead. Dead before they had a chance to mate.
RANDY	How do you know?
MILLIE	His song. He was still wooing her. Once he's got her approval, he quits singing her praises.
RANDY	I'd never do that.
MILLIE	I know.

Silence.
Randy picks up one of the birds.

RANDY	Would the Nature Centre want them?
MILLIE	It costs hundreds of dollars to stuff a hummingbird.
RANDY	I'd pay. It would be a legacy from us.
MILLIE	I think we should bury them.
RANDY	Only we would know where they are.
MILLIE	A gift to the earth from the Early Worm Club.
RANDY	Like a pledge?
MILLIE	You and me.

Sound of owl screeching once, then twice.
Millie smiles at Randy.
Music.
Blackout.

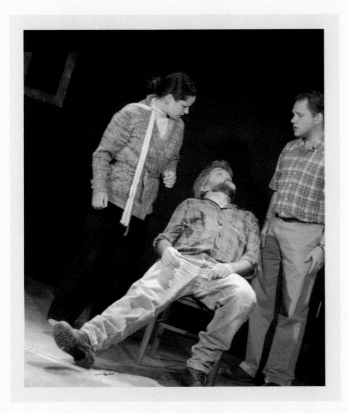

Abby's Place, FemFest:
Kami Desilets as Abby;
Randal Payne as Clyde;
Shawn Kowalke as Rodney.
Photo by Lynn Kohler.

ABBY'S PLACE

Abby's Place, FemFest: Kami Desilets as Abby and Shawn Kowalke as Rodney. Photo by Lynn Kohler.

Abby's Place was first produced by Sarasvàti Productions at FemFest! 2006: Breakin' Out, in Winnipeg, Manitoba, from 20 to 29 October 2006, with the following cast and crew:

CLYDE Randal Payne
RODNEY Shawn Kowalke
ABBY Kami Desilets

DIRECTOR Keri-lee Smith
STAGE MANAGER Ntara Curry
COSTUME / SETS Abby Myers
SOUND Ryan Morton

Characters

CLYDE, fifties, operates the summer village and town dump. He is a self-taught philosopher.

RODNEY, late thirties, a dentist in Edmonton. He has recently purchased a cottage that needs a lot of fixing as a retreat for himself and hospice for his wife.

ABBY, thirties, married to Rodney for ten years. Abby is used to solitude.

Time

The action follows nearly one year from early spring to early spring, 1990.

Place

Northern Alberta

Set

There is a hole or pit, a lowered area, where an actor can be unseen. The pit is also the lake in some sequences. The upper area, or edge of the pit, is also a deck or dock. An old shack is suggested in the upper playing space. There are areas of elevation from a low level outside the pit to the upper deck or edge. Actual objects of junk are not indicated. Except for the cellphone in scenes with Clyde, telephones are not represented. There are three matching wooden deck chairs.

Music

The soundscape can be performed by Clyde or a musician on or near the stage from found objects (brick, wood, glass, metal, paper, plastic), starting with low-sounding pitches at the beginning and funneling up to a tintinnabulation of beads, bells, and other high-pitched sounds by the end.

SCENE 1   Morning, early spring, at the dump

Music. Clyde blends in with the garbage in the pit, unseen by Rodney, who opens one of the bags he carries, takes out some old dishes and hurls them into the pit. Abby is lying with her back to the audience.

RODNEY   I always wanted to do this!

CLYDE   Hey!

RODNEY   Frisbee!

CLYDE   Ow! Cut it out!

RODNEY   What? Oh! . . . I didn't see you!

CLYDE   I got enough torments without a guy hurling garbage on my head.

RODNEY   It was just some old chipped plates! How would I know there was someone down there?

CLYDE   Yeah, up there in the land of the living you don't know a lot of things. Like to look before you throw stuff. Like how it feels when the pit gulps you alive. Like being a piece of living garbage.

Abby is on her back, looking up. She is breathing hard. Clyde emerges with bag of cans.

RODNEY   Do you . . . work here?

CLYDE   Well, I'm not on a picnic. Huh, I can tell by your truck that you live the sunlit life. Mine's over by my shack. I'm waiting for some parts to come in. Like a total replacement.

RODNEY   That might take some time.

CLYDE   Everything ends up here sooner or later.

RODNEY   Hey, someone put a good wood deck chair down there. Look at that.

CLYDE   Lookin's free.

RODNEY	Under those orange bags by the red carpet?
CLYDE	I . . . I don't see colours.
RODNEY	Could be still good.
CLYDE	I know what's comin'.
RODNEY	Could I see it?
CLYDE	I don't really feel like going back down there over your Granny's broken china.
RODNEY	I could.
CLYDE	No, I don't let anybody in the pit. I run a clean, safe dump.
RODNEY	My wife would like a chair like that.

Abby rolls over, her back to the audience.

CLYDE	What for?
RODNEY	I'm fixing up a cottage at the lake.
CLYDE	Oh, cottage, eh? You some university type?
RODNEY	I'm a dentist.
CLYDE	Huh. And they say I work in a sewer. Huh. You must have a complex.
RODNEY	What?
CLYDE	Everyone must hate your guts.
RODNEY	Not really.
CLYDE	For what you do to them, eh? And then how you make them pay.
RODNEY	The rates are all set by the government —
CLYDE	Don't get me started about the government, or I won't get anything done today.
RODNEY	What do you do here, anyway?
CLYDE	I look for pennies in the wishing well! Hah! See this bag? When I get a hundred cans, that's five bucks right there.

RODNEY	So you go through the bags for bottles. I hope you don't pour out the dregs and make a devil's brew!
CLYDE	Yeah, well, depends on if I'm drinking that day and what's in the refrigerator! Heh!
RODNEY	(*To himself*) Gross.
CLYDE	(*Climbing up*) Ya gotta be nuts to fix this. Rear leg's busted.
RODNEY	I've got a few tools . . .
CLYDE	Dollars to donuts you'll be bringing it back.

Clyde checks Rodney's bags and boxes.

RODNEY	Can I give you a few for hauling it out?
CLYDE	Well, you're not shopping for free. These old dishes should get me a few bucks, too, eh? Burns me when I see scoffers wrecking stuff for the hell of it.

Music. Clyde takes the bag into his shack. Rodney carries the chair to deck.

SCENE 2 The lake

Rodney speaks on the cellphone to Abby, who is still in the city. Abby sits cross-legged.

RODNEY	I've just got to make it livable. I don't want you doing anything when you get here. I've got the sink to fix yet.
ABBY	You're enjoying this, aren't you?
RODNEY	I love it. But I feel like I've lost so much time.
ABBY	I just keep looking ahead.
RODNEY	I'm really sure about this.
ABBY	I'm holding on to that.
RODNEY	This is a healing place.
ABBY	For one of us, maybe.

RODNEY	For us.
ABBY	Us.
RODNEY	Hang on, Abby. I'll call you later.
ABBY	I know.

Abby is down, hugging the ground.

SCENE 3 The dump, following weekend

Rodney carries lumber through mud and throws it in a pile. Clyde enters.

CLYDE	I see you've got a little bit of everything and not much of anything.
RODNEY	Yeah, just a bunch of junk from the old garage.
CLYDE	Hell of a rain, eh?
RODNEY	Yeah. Do you get that a lot up here?
CLYDE	All the time. Like a two-assed cow pissing on a flat rock.
RODNEY	(*Laughs*) I'll remember not to come out here after it rains. I can hardly move in this mud.
CLYDE	Ah, mud, dirt, it's all the same to me. Life is mud. It's what's poking up out of it, sparkling in the sun, that makes a life worth living.

Clyde pulls a push lawnmower out of the pile.
Abby, in her own space, slowly rouses and goes through some of the motions of life with the weight of her solitude.

RODNEY	(*Pause*) That's a relic you got there.
CLYDE	This shoulda been in the scrap metal pile.
RODNEY	Does anybody use those old hand-push kind anymore?
CLYDE	I got people lining up for these things. Look at that metal plating under there, eh?
RODNEY	Yeah.

CLYDE	These were made just after the war. Dandy units.
RODNEY	My wife would like a lawnmower like that.
CLYDE	Your wife again. If your wife likes my stuff so much, why doesn't she come out here and look for herself?
RODNEY	She likes quiet.
CLYDE	Nothing but quiet here. Just me and my junk.
RODNEY	I mean the lawnmower. It doesn't make much noise.
CLYDE	Yeah. It barely whispers. I got another one over by my shack, but it's spoken for. I keep all the stuff I can fix quick and sell fast.
RODNEY	You don't need that one, then.
CLYDE	I don't need it, but I'm going to keep it for parts.
RODNEY	Oh.
CLYDE	So what are you looking for?
RODNEY	Plumbing pipe? You got any?
CLYDE	Huh. A guy from up north, he comes in and pretty much fills my truck with his empties. All they do up there is work and drink, eh? Yeah, he just scooped your box of plumbing stuff yesterday.
RODNEY	So nothing for plumbing.
CLYDE	You running on septic?
RODNEY	Yeah.
CLYDE	If you want your tank emptied, my brother, he's got a honey wagon. He'll come suck her out. His name is Cal.
RODNEY	What's your name?
CLYDE	Clyde. Here's my card. I got the hours of the dump listed on there. Cal's number is on the back. If you call him, tell him I set you up. Maybe he'll bring me a hello for that.
RODNEY	Uh, they, uh, sucked out the septic before I moved in.
CLYDE	Oh. You got an outhouse?

RODNEY	Yeah, but it's pretty primitive.
CLYDE	If it stinks after you lime it, you'll need to get her sucked out, too. Twice a year.
RODNEY	I doubt it'll get that much use, actually.
CLYDE	If I just bought a place, I'd get the outhouse done. They just stick the nozzle down the hole and sucks her all out.
RODNEY	You and your brother must have a corner on the refuse business.

Abby stops, immobilized, collapses.

CLYDE	Yup. So. The wife won't use the biffy, eh?
RODNEY	I'd like to get the indoor plumbing ready for her.
CLYDE	Most women won't take the outhouse if you give them the choice, eh? Except my daughter, Dusty, now there's one who's more leather 'n lace. She works the rodeos . . . she don't come back here much.
RODNEY	So do you . . . live out here?
CLYDE	Yeah, I got my trailer, I got my shack. I had a dog once, Flytrap, but he run off. That was after the wife left me, praise the Lord. She couldn't abide with all the junk. I told her what the good book says: It's better to live on a desert island than with a wife like her.
RODNEY	It says that?
CLYDE	Oh, sure. Hell, I'd rather lie down between a lion and a dragon than listen to my wife. She was just like your leaky pipe, there. Drip, drip, drip.
RODNEY	Uh, so are you sure you don't have a spare p-trap?
CLYDE	Well . . . I could look in my grandaddy's magic drawer.
RODNEY	It's magic?
CLYDE	I call it that because it always has what I need. You should start one.

Clyde exits to his shack as Rodney moves away from pit.

SCENE 4   The lake, next weekend

Music. Abby moves to standing, a little desperate. She is still in the area identified as the city. Rodney speaks to her from the lake.

ABBY   Rodney?

RODNEY   Hi! I thought I'd take a break. Not used to all this fresh air and physical labour.

Abby continues to hold herself. She is listening but cannot reply.

RODNEY   Abby? Are you there?

ABBY   I'm still here.

RODNEY   So what did you do today? I tried calling earlier but you must have been out.

ABBY   I had an . . . incident.

RODNEY   Oh, no!

ABBY   It's because of all the meds they make me take.

RODNEY   What happened?

ABBY   I just blacked out.

RODNEY   Why didn't you call?

ABBY   I was unconscious, Rodney. When I woke up, I had to get to the hospital, and once I got there, I was busy, you know, and I didn't want to tell you until I knew what it was.

RODNEY   Well, what was it?

ABBY   They don't know. Maybe drug allergy.

RODNEY   You can't be alone. I've got to get home right away.

ABBY   You don't have to. They gave me something to help me sleep.

RODNEY   More meds. I just want to hold you.

ABBY   I'll be asleep.

RODNEY	I won't. I'm coming back tonight.
ABBY	No, it's too late to drive.
RODNEY	I have to.
ABBY	I have to sleep.
RODNEY	And I won't sleep until I've got you . . . here.

Beat. Music.
Rodney goes to Abby and leads her to the lake area.

RODNEY	Do you remember . . . after our wedding — all the guests and hotel staff, the taxi man, the airport, rental car people, even the awful radio in that car — we got to that cabin we'd rented and it felt like the first time in weeks we were alone. No one could reach us.
ABBY	No cellphones then. Bliss.
RODNEY	It's going to be like that here. Just us.
ABBY	I've been concentrating on just me for a long time now. So have you. Us seems like a lifetime ago.
RODNEY	This is for . . . you.
ABBY	The lake!

Abby sits in the deck chair.
Clyde sets up two more matching deck chairs with an old umbrella. Rodney gets his work gloves and a large bag of garbage. He puts a bottled beer in one of the gloves. He watches Abby before touching her goodbye. She is concentrating too hard to respond.

SCENE 5   The dump, a week later

Rodney carries the bag to the pit, waits a moment before throwing it in violently. Clyde watches him, lazing on one of his new deck chairs.

CLYDE	The wife here?
RODNEY	How did you know?
CLYDE	That's a pretty good deposit.

RODNEY	I just needed to make some noise.
CLYDE	You working hard today?
RODNEY	Not really.
CLYDE	I'm doin' a survey. This kinda heat slows ya down. (*Swats fly*) Most of us, anyway.
RODNEY	I brought you a beer.
CLYDE	Ohee. Just what a guy needs on a day like this. Hey, I got a full one I found in a batch of empties. Luck, eh? I put it in my fridge here to cool it off. (*Digging it out of the ground*) Ya never know what's going to rise up outta the dust o' the earth. That makes one for me and one for you.
RODNEY	I shouldn't stay. I . . .

Clyde opens beers, offering Rodney the buried one.

CLYDE	Whatsa matter?
RODNEY	A few flies today, eh? (*Swats*)
CLYDE	Yeah. Ya kill one and the rest come to the funeral.
RODNEY	Ha. By the way, here's your P-trap back and here's the one that leaks.
CLYDE	Didn't fit eh?
RODNEY	I had to buy a new one.
CLYDE	Full price?
RODNEY	Yeah, but it works.
CLYDE	So have a beer. Hey, how do you like my new umbrella? Just came in, eh? Take a load off.

Rodney reluctantly takes the beer.

RODNEY	Nice deck chairs. Same as the one I found.
CLYDE	Yup. Sometimes the Lord gives you back double what he takes away.

RODNEY	I have my doubts on that.
CLYDE	Well, look at these deck chairs and matching umbrella! You took the broken singleton and look what I end up with, eh? Perfect twins and a bonus!
RODNEY	Sure.

Rodney finally sits.

CLYDE	That's why it doesn't pay to be afraid. No use getting your shorts in a knot, eh Doc? 'Cause the Lord will send you just the package you don't want. Wouldn't be pain, otherwise, would it? 'Cause the thing you're most afraid of is what you're going to get.
RODNEY	Everyone is afraid of something.
CLYDE	You got that right. Like my little brother, Cliff. He worked the rigs like me, eh? Ah, but Cliffie, he's smarter, eh? So he gets sent out on one of them offshore rigs. Big bucks. It's like their own little island out there in the middle of the ocean. He sends me a letter, telling me about the pool tables, the movies, the computer games. So I sent him one. I says, "So how's the water?" Pulling his leg, eh? Tough big kid like that, but piss-scared of the water. He never wrote me back. You know why?
RODNEY	No.
CLYDE	Well, the rig, the whole works, she just dumped right over in this big Atlantic storm.
RODNEY	I remember that. The *Ocean Ranger*.
CLYDE	Yup. They all perished in that freezing water.
RODNEY	So even if he did know how to swim, it wouldn't have mattered.
CLYDE	Nope, but Lordy he musta been scared.
RODNEY	So you think if he wasn't scared, it wouldn't have happened?

CLYDE	Maybe not to him. Maybe he took that job to prove he wasn't. If he wasn't scared he just might not have taken it.
RODNEY	You think he was afraid to admit it.
CLYDE	I know so. Me, I'm a-scared of fire. One of the reasons I took this job. I gotta burn the pit regular. I'm working on my fear. I respect fire, eh, but I know I won't die by it. I'm not afraid of hell, either. I've read all the descriptions of hell in the Bible and guess what? It's just a dump like this. I figure I'm putting in my time now, eh, so I'm counting on going to heaven.

Abby drops her scarf or shawl.

RODNEY	I should call my wife.
CLYDE	You have my sympathies. You're on a short leash.
RODNEY	I just want to see if she's all right.
CLYDE	What are you afraid of?

Rodney uses cellphone. Music.

RODNEY	Everything okay?
ABBY	Fine.
CLYDE	Never seen one of them portables before.
RODNEY	I'm looking for a screen door, and then I'll be back.
ABBY	Rod?
RODNEY	Yeah?
ABBY	I can hear birds. Where are you?
RODNEY	Oh, it's an outdoor hardware store.
CLYDE	Hardware from hell.
ABBY	Bye.
CLYDE	Why didn't you tell her you were at the dump?
RODNEY	This is not her kind of place.

CLYDE	Maybe you're just making her up. Who ever heard of a wife like that?
RODNEY	She likes . . . fresh air.
CLYDE	Ah, you city types are too darned sensitive. I'll guarantee there's more pollution in your city streets on any given day than you'll find here at my dump.
RODNEY	She wants a screen door, to let the breeze in.
CLYDE	You just missed one the day before yesterday.
RODNEY	Too bad.
CLYDE	I can put you on the waiting list.
RODNEY	I'll give you my cell number, in case you get another one.
CLYDE	You can give me the number, but it won't do you any good. Screen doors get snapped up pretty quick, and besides, I don't own any kind of phone at all.
RODNEY	Well, you gave me your card, so have one of mine. (*Writes*) Here's our lot number, 78 on the summer village road.

Music. Rodney exits.

SCENE 6 The lake, a few weeks later

Clyde goes to cabin, bangs on door. Abby is still in the chair. She gathers herself to answer the door.

CLYDE	H-E-double toothpicks HELL!
ABBY	Hello?
CLYDE	Oh, s'cuse me. You must be the wife.
ABBY	Abby.
CLYDE	Hi, Abby. Ah!
ABBY	That looks really painful.

CLYDE	Swelled up like a poisoned gopher. I need the Doc.
ABBY	You mean Rodney?
CLYDE	It's an emergency.
ABBY	I can see that. Come in. I'll find him.
CLYDE	Come on, Doc, come on. I've been waiting for you all weekend.
ABBY	Rodney?

Alarmed that she's not where he left her, Rodney comes up from under the dock.

RODNEY	What is it? Clyde?
CLYDE	Ah, Doc, you gotta help me.
ABBY	How long has it been like this?
CLYDE	Three, four days.
RODNEY	Uh, we were just packing up.
ABBY	No hurry.
RODNEY	I can look at it, but I don't have any equipment here.
ABBY	Yes, we do. I brought my bag. I was going to throw it in the lake and make a wish or something. I'll get it.

Abby quickly gets the bag.

CLYDE	Hell, I just need ya to yank her out. Pair o' pliers will do.
RODNEY	All right, okay, let's stay outside . . . in the light.
CLYDE	See you got your screen door.
RODNEY	I . . . didn't think I'd hear from you.
ABBY	Quite swollen.
CLYDE	I don't always look this handsome.
ABBY	Gloves for you, Rod, and for me.
RODNEY	Are you sure?

ABBY	My patient.
CLYDE	Doc, aren't you doing this?
RODNEY	Abby and I used to be partners.
CLYDE	Uh, you don't want to get your hands dirty, m'am. My mouth is a history of my life.
ABBY	C'mon, Handsome. Open up. Uh-huh. Hm.
RODNEY	Oh, nasty.
ABBY	Missing a few, huh?
CLYDE	(*Mouth open*) Augh. (*Mouth closed*) Bar fight. Over a six-pack of sadness.
RODNEY	Anaesthetic.
CLYDE	The needle. I knew it. Doc, when do you take over here?
ABBY	This will hurt less than it does right now.
CLYDE	Go ahead. I'm not afraid.
ABBY	Done.
CLYDE	Didn't feel a thing. Hey, if you're so good at it, why'd you quit?
ABBY	Because I'm sick.
CLYDE	You don't look sick.
RODNEY	She's feeling better.
ABBY	I've been afraid to say it. I wish we didn't have to leave.
CLYDE	I was at a garage sale here once.
RODNEY	There will always be something to fix here.
ABBY	I like that you can say that: "There will always be . . ."
CLYDE	You've really cleaned it up.
RODNEY	I like to hear you say it.
ABBY	There will always be the lake.
CLYDE	My mouth feels funny.

ABBY	Then we're all set. Forceps.
RODNEY	There.
ABBY	Ugh. Ugh. Rod, help me.
CLYDE	(*Mouth open*) Doc!

Rodney takes over.

RODNEY	Just a little more twist, and there you are.
CLYDE	Agh. Ugh. Can I keep that?
RODNEY	Sure, I'll wrap it up for you.

Abby moves away, strips off gloves.

RODNEY	Are you all right?
ABBY	Time is falling out of my hands.

Clyde gets out of chair, seats Abby, takes the gloves from her.

CLYDE	Sit here. Nice job on the chair, Doc. Heh, it was in pieces when we found it.
ABBY	Oh? Where?
CLYDE	At the —
RODNEY	Where Clyde works.

Rodney shoves cotton gauze in Clyde's mouth.

RODNEY	Bite down on this.
CLYDE	(*Mouth closed*) The landfill site.
ABBY	I thought this chair came with the cabin.
RODNEY	Abby doesn't need to know.
CLYDE	(*Mouth open*) Why not? Truth is a healer. Falsehood is for fools.
ABBY	So there's life at the dump.

CLYDE	Sure there is. It's just dying to get out.
ABBY	The outdoor hardware?
RODNEY	Sometimes it's just easier finding something there than in town. I have to go there anyway to take the garbage.
ABBY	And Clyde's there.
CLYDE	Yeah, and I tell him what's what.
ABBY	I'm glad you came out here, Clyde, or we might never have met.
CLYDE	Yeah, well, I better take my rotten tooth here and get back to the pit. Let you folks get back to the city, too bad for you.

Clyde exits.

RODNEY	That was beautiful. Seeing you in action again.
ABBY	Let's stay. Please. Rod?
RODNEY	I'll call. I'll cancel my appointments for another week.

Rodney and Abby touch, tentatively.

SCENE 7 The dump, next weekend, day

Music. Abby goes to the dump, alone. Clyde is working on the lawnmower and continues as they talk.

ABBY	Hey, Clyde!
CLYDE	There. See. On a day nothing good happens, who'da thought Abby would come to see me? Where's the Doc?
ABBY	Rodney's at the cabin. Busy with pieces of something. Just like you.
CLYDE	Got piles of stuff like this. Spend a half hour on it and sell it for fifty bucks.

ABBY	I see the swelling has gone down.
CLYDE	What? Oh! Yeah. Healed up fine.

Abby looks around.

ABBY	So this is what it's like.
CLYDE	What? Oh, the dump.
ABBY	It's full of . . . things.
CLYDE	Yup. For me to salvage and fix.
ABBY	It's a lot of . . . stuff.
CLYDE	Oh, yeah. When the junk gets to me, I burn it. Mind you, it has to really pile up, eh, on account of my aversion to fire. I gotta really smell it bad before I burn, and considering I hardly have the sense of smell any more, I usually rely on complaints from town to know when it's time.
ABBY	Oh. (*Sits*) Hey, these chairs match the one I have!
CLYDE	Uh-huh?
ABBY	Oh! I mean, I just noticed them. I don't mean I want them.
CLYDE	I owe you for the tooth.
ABBY	I couldn't even finish the job.
CLYDE	But you opened the door.
ABBY	Maybe you'll open one for me.

Sound to indicate cellphone ringing.

CLYDE	Hah! He found you!
ABBY	Oh! Hi.
RODNEY	Are you on your way?
ABBY	Just now.
RODNEY	I'll get lunch ready, then.

ABBY	Home soon.
RODNEY	Okay.
ABBY	Bye. (*To Clyde*) He gets lonely.
CLYDE	No kids, eh?
ABBY	No. We thought we'd wait. And now . . . no chance.
CLYDE	The sickness, eh? I been sick before. Used to drink too much. Brought it on myself.
ABBY	Then you know how it's always there, like some grief that won't go away.
CLYDE	Like living at a dump. You either fight it or you accept it.
ABBY	It wants to wad me up inside and suffocate me in the hollow.
CLYDE	You can't let it.
ABBY	I know. Rodney isn't ready.
CLYDE	I never had no care what happened to me. Thing was, no one else did, either. Not my brothers, or my ex-wife, or even my daughter. S'why I did it maybe, to spite them all! But the Lord has given me a good view for all the remaining days of my life of where I've been, and for that I give thanks. I figure I'm stuck here forever, because the minute I move away from the pit, I'll forget what it was like and I'll fall right back in. This here dump is my life insurance policy.
ABBY	The lake is mine. And if it can't save me, it will save Rodney.
CLYDE	It gives him something to do.
ABBY	(*Pause*) I bet he'd like that old lawnmower.
CLYDE	I know he would.
ABBY	How much?
CLYDE	For you —
ABBY	I want to buy it. For Rodney's birthday.

CLYDE	Okay.
ABBY	I couldn't face going into a store, even in town. I —
CLYDE	For you, ten bucks. Normally, they're twenty.
ABBY	I've got it. Here.
CLYDE	He'll like it.
ABBY	He doesn't expect anything.
CLYDE	He'll laugh, then.
ABBY	Yeah.
CLYDE	You'd better get back to getting better. I'll deliver this later. I want to shine it up a bit for you. Might even giftwrap it!
ABBY	Clyde —
CLYDE	Yeah?
ABBY	It's good to know you're always here, I mean, in case we need repairs.
CLYDE	Oh, I'm a lifer, like I told you. I'm selling this as is, no warranty! But hell, if it's lasted this long it must be worth it, eh?
ABBY	Yeah. See you later.

Music. Abby goes to lake area.

SCENE 8 The lake, later

Music. Rodney invites Abby to dance, as if swimming, floating on the water. Clyde brings lawnmower to the deck, where he watches Rodney and Abby. He waits a bit to see if they notice him. He sets up the lawnmower and polishes it.

ABBY	I feel like I'm a part of everything here.
RODNEY	Just float.
ABBY	I want to say it. I have to make the effort now, or you won't be able to find me later.

RODNEY	Okay.
ABBY	I'm echoing across the lake.
RODNEY	I'm listening.
ABBY	In the city it's like I'm in brackets — not working, not producing, not contributing — but here it's the lake and us and the cabin. No jobs, no past, no people.

Rodney holds Abby.
Clyde takes a tattered bow out of his pocket, and ties it on the lawnmower but then stuffs it back in his pocket and leaves, unseen by Rodney and Abby.

RODNEY	Let's go swimming every day.
ABBY	Let's just be for now.
RODNEY	We both said it. Let's. Let us.
ABBY	I promise that if there is any way of reaching you, this is where I'll be. In the morning, when you go out on the dock to greet the lake, you can wave at me, and I'll wave back.

Music. They dance. Just as the dance is about to conclude, Abby lets go, worried, disturbed. Rodney disengages and goes to the dump in a hurry.

SCENE 9   The dump, next weekend, night

Rodney searches shack, ravine for Clyde. He wears a dental face mask to avoid breathing smoke and uses a flashlight.

RODNEY	Hey, Clyde! Where are you, you old hermit! I've searched the shack and the trailer. I hope you're not down the ravine. The wind's blowing that way!

Rodney, walking backwards, nearly slips into pit.

	What a place to pass out! Hey Clyde, wake up. C'mon.
CLYDE	Okay, okay! Oh, my poor brains!

RODNEY	I thought you were toast.
CLYDE	What's burning?
RODNEY	You got a fire near the ravine.
CLYDE	Now why'd they have to go and do that?
RODNEY	Who?
CLYDE	Mischief makers. They started fooling around with my special stash over there, chucking all my car batteries into the pit. I thought I finally scared them out of here, but I must have fallen and passed out.
RODNEY	You think they started it on purpose?
CLYDE	Oh, sure. They got something against me. They call me the Junkman.
RODNEY	Has this happened before? The fire chief didn't sound too worried.
CLYDE	Oh sure. Nothing new. And what's out here, eh? Just me and my junk. Who cares?
RODNEY	Well, I do. I came out here to find you, didn't I?
CLYDE	Yeah. Here we are again, you and me: an iron kettle and a clay pot tied up in the same bag.
RODNEY	What do you mean? Come on, get up.

Rodney folds up the umbrella and uses it to pull Clyde up out of the pit.

CLYDE	I mean, when the bag drops, which one of us is gonna end up in pieces?
RODNEY	You're going to be okay. You just need a big cup of coffee. And maybe a dip in the lake. Let's go see Abby.
CLYDE	Nah. It's the middle of the night.
RODNEY	She's the one who saw the smoke all the way to the lake. She'll be waiting up for us.
CLYDE	Okay, for Abby. Let's take these deck chairs with us. They didn't get burnt, so they musta been saved for her.

Clyde and Rodney take the chairs to the deck.

SCENE 10   The cabin, a few weeks later

Abby, Clyde, and Rodney sit on the three chairs.

CLYDE	Abby don't look like she wants to go home.
ABBY	Clyde is a mind reader.
RODNEY	Well, I've got to get back to work, right? I've taken off as much time as I could.
CLYDE	So why can't Abby stay while hubby goes back and forth?
RODNEY	No. I don't want her out here alone.
CLYDE	Don't you have neighbours?
RODNEY	Nobody stays out all week.
CLYDE	I'm here. Me and my mental telepathy.
ABBY	I don't get that tumbling feeling here, Rod.
RODNEY	I know you're better here but I . . .
CLYDE	He's just a-scared of you needing someone and no one's around.
ABBY	What about the cellphone? If Clyde kept it, I'd have a lifeline.
CLYDE	Me? The magician phone?
RODNEY	I don't know if Clyde could. . . .
CLYDE	What does this thing run on anyway? Solar?
ABBY	It has a battery charger you just plug in.
CLYDE	I don't have electric at my trailer.
RODNEY	Well, that's it, then.
CLYDE	As a rule, I don't like new things, eh? They haven't been held in the hand long enough.

ABBY	Oh, that one has.
CLYDE	But I suppose I could power it off my cigarette lighter overnight. I wonder if there's enough juice?
ABBY	You did that once, Rod. Remember when you stayed over with me at the hospital that time?
RODNEY	Yeah, that worked.
CLYDE	I got plenty of car batteries. And I got all your numbers here on this card you gave me.
RODNEY	But what about at night?
ABBY	At night we're asleep and we don't worry about each other and there's nothing anybody can do anyway wherever we are.

Abby takes the shawl from the chair and wraps it around herself.

CLYDE	Being close to the water is good for getting better.
ABBY	I like to watch the boats. Not the speed boats, but the fishing dinghies, when the lake is calm. The boats are anchored, secure, as if there's solid ground around them, not water. The fishermen stand; their silhouettes are still. They look like they could step out and walk across to me. But sometimes, if I shift my gaze to the sunset or the birds in the air, just for a moment, the boat is gone. Vanished, silent and secret, like a dream.
CLYDE	I'll make sure she keeps one foot on the ground, Doc.
RODNEY	You're sure.
CLYDE	Don't worry, there's nothing in the refrigerator.
RODNEY	I was wondering about that. Who's taking care of whom?
ABBY	I'll call you tonight, Clyde.
RODNEY	*(To Abby)* And I'll call you. Are you sure about this?
ABBY	This place is my lifeboat.

Clyde moves back to the dump.

CLYDE	(*Presses numbers*) Wish I had someone I could call.

Rodney exits.

SCENE 11 The trailer, weeks later

Music. Clyde is at the dump. Abby sits on the middle chair on the deck. Rodney paces, restless in the city, trying to get Abby's attention.

CLYDE	Pork 'n' beans tonight. What did you have?
ABBY	He always asks that. He thinks I won't eat if he's not here to cook for me.
CLYDE	How many times did he call today?
ABBY	Six.
CLYDE	Well, that's better than yesterday, anyway.
ABBY	I guess.
CLYDE	You have to give him time to let go, little by little.
ABBY	I don't have time.
CLYDE	He'll learn.
ABBY	I like talking to you.
CLYDE	I'm just doing my job.
ABBY	So, how did you sleep last night?
CLYDE	Well, not much, eh? Too wound up. It's not like I don't get enough fresh air or nothing, out at the dump all day. Probably not enough exercise. Used to work the rigs. Slept hard then, eh?
ABBY	I like to watch the spiders at night. What do you do when you can't sleep?
CLYDE	Once upon a time I'd have a drink. But now, I sit up. I read. What I'm doing right now. Full moon, enough light to read by. Only thing is the fool bats out here.

Wish to heaven they'd leave me alone. Got hit by one once, it musta been drunk on fermented berries. Oooh. Didn't like that. Bats are mice with wings, eh? I like 'em on the ground where I can step on 'em, not flicking around my ears.

ABBY   The trick with bats is to sit still, like a tree. Keep your shirt tucked in, so nothing's flapping in the wind.

CLYDE   I'll try that.

ABBY   What are you reading?

CLYDE   *The Book of Wisdom.*

ABBY   Yeah?

CLYDE   Yeah, I read a bit and then I think a bit. I'm studying my life. Trying to figure out why I ended up at the dump. I guess I had no other place to go. But listen to me now, eh? Talking on a cellular with my phone pal Abby every night. I must be doing something right.

ABBY   Goodnight, Clyde.

CLYDE   'Night, Abby.

RODNEY   Abby? The phone was busy. Are you okay?

Music.

SCENE 12   The lake

Rodney moves to Abby at the lake, waits. Clyde retires into his shack.

ABBY   What's the matter?

RODNEY   Do you want to go out in the boat today?

ABBY   No, I'm happy sitting here.

RODNEY   Is there anything else you want to do?

ABBY   No, really. I'm fine.

RODNEY	A walk, maybe?
ABBY	Maybe later, when it cools off.
RODNEY	I feel like we should do something together. We don't eat at the same times anymore. Or sleep. You've got your own schedule . . .
ABBY	It's blank, Rodney.
RODNEY	You're alone so much.
ABBY	I can focus better that way.
RODNEY	I need to be with you.
ABBY	I know you're thinking of me. Watching me.
RODNEY	But if I get too close it's like you have trouble breathing.
ABBY	It breaks my concentration.
RODNEY	I wish I could help you.
ABBY	I know.
RODNEY	Maybe a walk later when it's cooler, then?
ABBY	Maybe.

Rodney goes to fix something under the deck. Clyde finds him, avoids Abby, who is meditative.

RODNEY	Clyde!
CLYDE	Hey! Let me hold that for you.

Rodney hammers.

RODNEY	I want to reinforce this deck. Abby spends so much time on it.
CLYDE	Don't want her to fall.
RODNEY	(*Nail in mouth*) Uh-uh.
CLYDE	You're the one who should worry about falling.

RODNEY	As long as I keep my hands busy, I'm okay.
CLYDE	Keep nailing, then.
RODNEY	Did she see you're here?
CLYDE	She doesn't need to know.
RODNEY	What's wrong?
CLYDE	It's the phone calls.
RODNEY	From you?
CLYDE	No, from you, Doc.
RODNEY	She told you this?
CLYDE	When you're in the city you're calling her eight, nine times a day.
RODNEY	She hardly ever phones me.
CLYDE	You're not giving her a chance. She phones me every night.
RODNEY	She does?
CLYDE	Yeah, she makes sure I'm reading my Bible.
RODNEY	She's looking after you, then.
CLYDE	She thinks so.
RODNEY	So she would rather talk to you. How's that supposed to make me feel?
CLYDE	Hey, Doc. I'm nothing, a big, hollow zero. Maybe that's easier for her, because I don't count for much.
RODNEY	Look at her out there. She's so calm. How does she do that?
CLYDE	She's breathing with the lake.

Abby sits on edge of deck, feet dangling.

RODNEY	So what do I do?

Clyde takes out cellphone.

CLYDE   This old thing does the long distance, eh?

RODNEY   Yeah.

CLYDE   Like this. (*To phone*) Hiya, Doc! Same as always. Uh,
          how's the weather? (*Peeking out under the deck*) Sun
          is shining, sort of. The lake is still there. She's still
          looking at it. (*Prompt to Rodney*) How's the fishing?

RODNEY   How's the fishing?

CLYDE   Yeah, got a few the other day. Tried out the phone
          from my boat, which I finally got patched up and
          painted. Gave her a name, too, for good luck, eh?
          The Abigail. Even checked my Bible for the spelling.
          Called up Abby from the middle o' the lake. It was
          like she walked out on the water and sat down on
          the bow. "Hi Clyde." That clear. She doesn't say much,
          hell, how could she with me bursting with ways to
          change the world on the other end of this honker?

RODNEY   Okay, okay. I'll check in with you sometimes if I get . . .
          anxious.

CLYDE   Remember, I'm in the salvage business. My whole life,
          in fact, is a salvage operation.

RODNEY   That's what I admire about you. 'Cause I don't know
          how I'm . . . I don't like this. I don't like leaving her
          alone so much.

CLYDE   I told her that. I gave her a piece of Psalm 28. It goes,
          "If you are silent to me, I shall be like those who go
          down to the Pit."

RODNEY   I'm going to cancel Fridays at the office for the rest of
          the summer.

Rodney takes phone, turns it off, and hands it back to Clyde.
Abby leans back with a sigh of relief.

SCENE 13   The dump, early fall

Music. Clyde goes up to the dump, on the far edge of the pit nearest to the ravine. Rodney and Abby carry a large green garbage bag to the dump. They stay on the side of the pit opposite to Clyde.

RODNEY	Clyde! What a mud pie!
CLYDE	Yeah. Good weather if you're a duck.
RODNEY	We better stay over here on the high ground.
CLYDE	You do that. This mud sucks you up if you let it. It sucks up your soul.
RODNEY	Not too busy today, eh?
CLYDE	Ah, nobody comes out in this.
ABBY	Most people have closed up already.
CLYDE	Yeah, summer's over.
ABBY	It's almost winter!
CLYDE	Yeah, I'm alone out here with my empty pit for the duration. Burned the dump for the last time.
ABBY	You mean until spring.
CLYDE	Ah, who knows if I'll last that long. Here, catch!

Clyde tosses the phone to Rodney.

RODNEY	Whoa! No, Clyde, we want you to keep it.
CLYDE	What for?
RODNEY	Well, you need it.
ABBY	So we can call you and find out when it's spring.

Rodney throws the phone to Clyde.

CLYDE	But it must be worth something, eh?
RODNEY	It's a gift.

ABBY	In case you have any more trouble around here.
CLYDE	Could come in handy, all right.
RODNEY	If I take it back, I'll use it too much.
CLYDE	If I had a phone, I could sign up for search and rescue.
RODNEY	You'd be really good at that.
CLYDE	Yeah. There's always a few characters who get lost in the bush in the winter. Being colourblind is an advantage with the snow, eh? I see lights and darks better. I can see things that are out of place.
ABBY	Like what is sticking up out of the mud.
RODNEY	This is for you, too. (*Throws bag over*)
CLYDE	Empties?
RODNEY	A hundred to a bag. A whole summer's worth.
CLYDE	I appreciate that.
RODNEY	We should go. So long, Clyde!
ABBY	Bye, Clyde.

Abby drops her scarf in the pit, not noticed by Rodney or Clyde.

CLYDE	See ya in the spring!

Rodney and Abby exit.

SCENE 14   The dump, late winter

Clyde talks on the cellphone to the fire chief.

CLYDE	Hey, Chief! Yeah, well, strike at the shepherd and the sheep will scatter, eh? I just told him you'd be waiting at the bottom of the road. They headed down the ravine on them three-wheeled donor cycles, heh, got that? Donor cycles? Anyway, yeah, I'd like to be paid for my gas. Sure, he can pay me in empties. You're

gonna make him pick cans out of the ditch? Why not? Probably theirs, anyways. Yeah, young once, yeah, long time ago. You know, I wouldn't mind trying out one of those . . . three-wheeled units. You think so, eh? Well, naw, I like to have something around me when I'm driving. Yeah. Don't like being exposed, you know, on the road, but I wouldn't mind bombing around on one in the bush for a day. Sure, ask him. He'll say no, but you can ask. That or get grounded, eh? Well, whatever you say. Sure, Chief. Yeah, excellent. You bet.

Clyde puts the phone in his pocket.

SCENE 15 The dump, spring

Music. The pit is smoking. Rodney enters from the lowest level, picks up some stones, and throws them in the pit with gathering intensity throughout. Clyde enters from shack.

CLYDE   Well, I'll be damnified! I hardly seen you through the smoke.

RODNEY   Hi.

CLYDE   She's burning good, eh?

RODNEY   Yeah.

CLYDE   I haven't heard from you guys since Christmas. That made my day, getting that call from Abby. Hey, did she come up this weekend?

RODNEY   No. She . . .

CLYDE   Bit cold yet, eh? Hey! I gotta tell her about this chinook we had in the middle of March, and everybody's got spring fever, uh? I'm in the shack flat on the floor like Humpty Dumpty, eh, but I can hear through my brain haze that my little arsonists are outside. My mind is doing wheelies, and my eyes are like two pee holes in the snow . . . oh, Lordy . . . but I seen them go to my truck and siphon off some gasoline (I got the old putt-putt working this winter, eh?) and then they throw the whole works on an old car chassis in the metal pile, and they light her up! So I get the phone, and I call my pal the fire chief — I know him real well now 'cause we're on search and rescue together — and I recognize one of those knotheads out there is his kid! — so his ass is in boiling hot water . . .

Rodney sees scarf, reaches for it, falls into the pit.

CLYDE   Hey, Doc! Watch out!

RODNEY   Damn!

Clyde goes around the pit to Rodney.

CLYDE   What are you doing?

RODNEY   I slipped!

CLYDE   What in the hell —

RODNEY   It's Abby's. It's her colour. I don't want it to burn.

Rodney gets the scarf, but burns his hand, and wraps the scarf around it.

CLYDE   Come on out of there!

RODNEY   I'm trying!

CLYDE   You'll burn yourself!

RODNEY   I keep sliding!

CLYDE   Just put one foot in front of the other!

RODNEY   It's not that easy in this slush.

CLYDE   No wonder! You don't have any boots on!

Rodney tries to get up again and collapses.

RODNEY   Clyde. She's gone.

CLYDE   (*Pause*) Gone?

RODNEY   She died!

CLYDE   (*Pause*) Oh, Doc. (*Pause*) Oh, I'm sorry to hear that.

RODNEY	I had to come out here.
CLYDE	Get on up out of there, now.

Rodney tries to get up.

RODNEY	I can't.
CLYDE	Don't be a fool.
RODNEY	It hurts like hell.
CLYDE	You gotta get up.
RODNEY	What for?
CLYDE	You gotta go back to the lake.
RODNEY	Why?
CLYDE	'Cause it helped Abby!
RODNEY	The lake sucked me into thinking she was better!
CLYDE	She was.
RODNEY	But she died.
CLYDE	Yeah. (*Pause*) Give me your hand. C'mon, Doc. Doc?

Clyde pulls Rodney out. Abby rises out of the pit behind Rodney and circles her way around it, and around the men, and makes her way to the deck.

RODNEY	I didn't know where else to go.
CLYDE	It's okay. You got to do your howling someplace.
RODNEY	Yeah.
CLYDE	It's good you came.
RODNEY	She wanted the three of us to sit outside one night as soon as it was warm.
CLYDE	Well then, we'll do that. You go make peace with the lake, then I'll come over some night and I'll sit and drink beer with you. And we'll talk about her, so she'll be there, too . . . uh, never mind I'm scared of bats, eh? Abby was going to help me work on that.

| RODNEY | I'd like to know what she saw out there. |

Abby is on the deck, in the middle chair, in her former pose.

ABBY	There will always be the lake.
RODNEY	She called me the day she went.
ABBY	Rodney. Come home. I'll wait.
RODNEY	And she did.
CLYDE	She sure knew her own way.
RODNEY	I'm going to go . . . and open up the cabin . . . and clean up those dump chairs, and we'll sit and talk about her.

Rodney and Clyde go to the deck.

CLYDE	No, leave them chairs how they are, spider webs and all. She liked to watch the spiders, she told me. Never met a woman like her.
RODNEY	Yeah. Stuff like that. Everything we can remember.
CLYDE	I'll bring the beer.

Rodney and Clyde sit, Abby between them, for a moment. Then she dances, into the water, and waves.

RODNEY	We'll go fishing.
CLYDE	I got a lucky boat.
RODNEY	I'll call you.
CLYDE	Yup. You do that, buddy.

Music. Fade to black.

The Seed Savers,
Station Arts Centre:
Will Brooks as Solo and
Carmela Sison as Sky.
Photo by Michael Clark.

The
SEED SAVERS

The Seed Savers, Workshop West Theatre: David MacInnis as Solo and Natasha Napoleao as Sky.
Photo by Russ Hewitt.

The Seed Savers was first produced at Workshop West Theatre, in Edmonton, Alberta, from 29 October to 8 November 2009, with the following cast and crew:

MINDY Maralyn Ryan
JOE John Wright
SKY Natasha Napoleao
SOLO David MacInnis
TYLER Jesse Gervais

DIRECTOR Michael Clark
SET AND LIGHTING DESIGN April Viczko
COSTUME DESIGN Daniela Masellis
MUSIC AND SOUND DESIGN Paul Morgan Donald
CHOREOGRAPHY Amber Borotsik
STAGE MANAGER Anna Davidson
PRODUCTION MANAGER Ben Eastep
TECHNICIANS Eric Chamberlin and Erik Martin
PUBLICITY Fat Cat Media Relations

The Seed Savers was revised and produced at Station Arts Centre, in Rosthern, Saskatchewan, from 1 July to 1 August 2010, with the following cast and crew:

MINDY Sharon Bakker
JOE Kent Allen
SKY Carmela Sison
SOLO Will Brooks
TYLER Matt Josdal

DIRECTOR Michael Clark
SET DESIGN Hans Becker
LIGHTING DESIGN Tim Cardinal
COSTUME DESIGN Theresa Germain
MUSIC AND SOUND DESIGN Paul Morgan Donald
STAGE MANAGER Diana Domm
TECHNICIAN Craig Langlois

Characters
MINDY, Joe's wife for fifty years, an earthy woman
JOE, late sixties, a farmer, successful, but not a stranger to hard times
SOLO, mid-twenties, farmer, has a few years of agricultural college
SKY, mid-twenties, Mindy and Joe's granddaughter, of mixed race heritage
TYLER, mid-twenties, local boy now but not always, salesman for a multinational
    chemical and seed company

Time
1998–99
Act 1: Late summer to late fall
Act 2: Late fall to late summer

Place
The prairie, near a small town

Set
The set is bare except for a few props as indicated. The suggestion of a rolling
prairie vista, a pond, and an elevated space indicating the dream bed, are
required.

THE DREAM BED is a remote and secret place, a high narrow ledge on top of
a hill. Dug out and lined with special rocks, it is a place for fasting, dreaming,
and vision quests.

THE WIND, the life force, is indicated by sound, music, light, movement, or
some combination of design elements.

Sound
Aeolian harp or wind chimes or contemporary naturalistic music

Scenes
Note: Scene titles are for identification only.

PROLOGUE Windsong

Act One
SCENE 1 Work of the Wind
SCENE 2 Truck Tour
SCENE 3 Candlelight Dinner
SCENE 4 Apron of Many Pockets
SCENE 5 Beer Buddies
SCENE 6 The Letter
SCENE 7 Dream Bed

Act Two
SCENE 1 Anniversary
SCENE 2 Winter
SCENE 3 Sales Call
SCENE 4 Planting Trees
SCENE 5 Desert
SCENE 6 Truck Tour Two
SCENE 7 Moving On Up
SCENE 8 Field Check
SCENE 9 First Crop
SCENE 10 Supreme Court

EPILOGUE Song of Songs

Whoever said that farming is the foundation of all the arts is quite correct. When all is well on the farms, all is well elsewhere.

— XENOPHON, *Oeconomicus*, c. 370 BC

PROLOGUE Windsong

Mindy enters. Sound of the birds. It's early sunrise, in the yard. Mindy throws some seeds for the birds. Sound of wind, taunting.

MINDY   Oh, you. Plenty for you, too.

Mindy throws some seeds to the wind.

MINDY   Take it! Go on! Even though you don't need it. For life.

Joe approaches, but Mindy does not see.

MINDY   How do you live without seed?

JOE (*off*)   Mindy!

MINDY   All you have are songs. Singing, always singing, like a lost bird!

JOE (*off*)   Min?

MINDY   They say the northwest wind makes you wise.

JOE (*off*)   Min!

Sound of wind, travelling.

MINDY   Oh! Go on, then. But I'm not giving up on you!

ACT ONE

SCENE 1 Work of the Wind

Joe enters the yard.

JOE	You talking to the wind again?
MINDY	It tells me things.
JOE	It tell you it's gonna rain?
MINDY	There's something more, today.
JOE	Before it pours, I could use some tea.
MINDY	What's going on?
JOE	The air is full is all.
MINDY	I got no time for tea.

Beat.

JOE	I saw the heron by the dugout.
MINDY	Oh? Flying or fishing?
JOE	Flying. Agitated, like.
MINDY	Like you.
JOE	Circling.
MINDY	He knows.
JOE	Hah! King of the sky. He's just a hungry heron. Hungry, like I'm thirsty.
MINDY	Some king you are.
JOE	Is that what the wind says.
MINDY	Joe. Who's coming?
JOE	Rain. Probably hail, too.
MINDY	If it's the girls and the kids up from Regina, I'll have to get some rolls in the oven.

JOE	Not the kids, thank the Lord.
MINDY	Who, then?
JOE	Not sure.
MINDY	Someone who wants to help?
JOE	Who in their right mind would show up at harvest time?
MINDY	It's someone I know.
JOE	If you know so much, why are you asking?
MINDY	I'll figure you out yet.
JOE	I'm dried right out. I need my tea!
MINDY	We see everyone at Christmas and Easter. The only ones who never come are . . . "King of the sky." It's Sky!
JOE	She called, is all.
MINDY	Sky phoned us?
JOE	Yeah.
MINDY	When?
JOE	You were busy.
MINDY	What on earth was I doing?
JOE	Boiling water.
MINDY	For your tea?
JOE	In your big vat.
MINDY	I was canning?
JOE	You don't like getting startled when you're canning.
MINDY	My granddaughter calls from Toronto after all this time and you don't tell me for a whole week?
JOE	I didn't want you to bubble over.
MINDY	Is Sky all right?
JOE	She's okay.
MINDY	She's never called before.

JOE	We got that one letter, with the map, but after that, not even a bloody card!

Beat.

MINDY	Why did she call?
JOE	Just to chitchat.
MINDY	Lord love a duck.
JOE	You know, shoot the breeze.
MINDY	What did she say?

Beat.

JOE	She asked about the farm.
MINDY	The farm?
JOE	Summers here as a kid. She misses it.
MINDY	That's a miracle. Her father hated it.
JOE	She's got a few bones to pick, too.
MINDY	She's got a few bones to pick with you!
JOE	There. That's why I kept a lid on it.
MINDY	Davey hated us in the end.
JOE	She's got questions about him.
MINDY	So do I.
JOE	Can of worms.
MINDY	I could just ring your neck.
JOE	Then I won't have to talk.

Beat.

MINDY	Did she ask about me?
JOE	You were up to your neck in pickles!
MINDY	I should have talked to her! If you do this again, Joe Brandt, you will die alone!

Beat.

JOE	She called about her mother.
MINDY	What about her.
JOE	She's dead.
MINDY	Dead!
JOE	Got hit by a car. On that, uh, King Street.
MINDY	Oh, my Lord.
JOE	Killed on impact.
MINDY	That's why she called.
JOE	Death at harvest.
MINDY	You don't keep life-and-death secrets from me!
JOE	I'd just started swathing!
MINDY	I need to go there.
JOE	Not there.
MINDY	You can't stop me.
JOE	The ravine.
MINDY	Her, too?

Beat.

JOE	Together at last.
MINDY	Our son should have been laid to rest here, not scattered in a city ravine.
JOE	She was the wife.
MINDY	She abandoned Davey!
JOE	And us.
MINDY	Well, she can't keep us away from Sky now.
JOE	Sky's got her mother in her. That woman came and went like the weather. And took Davey and Sky with her.

MINDY	It's the worst thing for a girl to lose her mother!
JOE	Hope she had the sense to grow up, like her father never did.
MINDY	We're going to Toronto.
JOE	We can't.
MINDY	To comfort our granddaughter.
JOE	She won't be there.

Beat.

MINDY	Sky is coming?
JOE	It's up in the air. Like my cup of tea.
MINDY	You asked her.
JOE	For a visit, like.
MINDY	I don't know whether to hug you or hammer you!
JOE	Just don't go making a mountain of bread.
MINDY	Oh, for Sky, something more exotic.
JOE	Now she's the Queen of Sheba.
MINDY	Stollen! Apples and nuts and cinnamon.
JOE	Just don't go scaring her off.
MINDY	Tomorrow? In a few days?
JOE	I left it wide open.
MINDY	This is why I listen to the wind.
JOE	I can't stop long with the clouds loading up.
MINDY	Go! Get it all done before she gets here!
JOE	Fifty years and I gotta make my own damned tea.

Joe exits. Sound of rain.

MINDY	(*To off*) Joe! Did you tell her about the party?

JOE (*off*)	I might have mentioned it.
MINDY	Did she say she'll stay? Joe?
JOE (*off*)	I wasn't sure of the date.

Mindy exits. Sound of wind.

MINDY (*off*)	Joe! October twenty-third! How come you don't know that?
JOE (*off*)	I knew that!
MINDY (*off*)	Oh, get out of my way. Let me do it!

Rain stops. Music.
Sky enters with two rolling suitcases.
Sky takes in the colours, the sounds and smells of fall on the farm. She lets the wind play in her hair, her face, lifts her arms and gives in to it. For the first time in a long time, she's home.

| SKY | "Your name is perfume poured out." |

Sound of wind, animated.
Music.

SCENE 2   Truck Tour

| MINDY (*off*) | Lunch will be ready soon. Don't be long. |

Joe enters.

JOE	(*To off*) Just showing Sky the lay of the land.
SKY	She's just like I remember her.
JOE	Your Grandma wants you all to herself.
SKY	Does she still bake three desserts for lunch?
JOE	To her, you're the lost sheep.
SKY	Lost? (*Pause*) You sent us away.
JOE	I didn't mean forever!

SKY	He was never coming back.
JOE	He needed help.
SKY	He never got it.
JOE	Did your mother try?
SKY	He refused. She gave up.
JOE	And you?
SKY	I couldn't.
JOE	Means the world that you came out here.
SKY	Law school trains you to look at a question from all angles.
JOE	You had lots of time to think.
SKY	You put me in exile!
JOE	You weren't exactly in the desert.
SKY	Well, no.

Joe pulls out a pouch from his pocket.

JOE	I've spent time in the desert. I got this in Egypt.
SKY	Is it sand?
JOE	No. . . . Wheat.
SKY	What's it for?
JOE	It's a gift. From a shrivelled up farmer, old as the hills.
SKY	I never knew you went to Egypt.

Joe pockets the pouch.

JOE	Ages ago. Before we met your mother.
SKY	Mom only dreamed of going to Egypt. To commune with the ancestors.
JOE	And you?
SKY	I can't wait to meet my little cousins.
JOE	Mindy's over the moon that you're staying for the party.

SKY	Only if I can help out.
JOE	She'll be baking buns to feed the whole district.
SKY	I mean, with the harvest.
JOE	You want to help me?
SKY	I'm not afraid of work.
JOE	Not driving tractor.
SKY	I've learned how to drive.
JOE	I don't know. New tractor.
SKY	What about the truck?
JOE	Hauling grain?
SKY	The big red one?
JOE	That old geezer takes a strong hand.
SKY	I can do it.
JOE	Son of a gun.
SKY	When do I start?
JOE	Gonna need a steady wind to sop up all this moisture. The north field is a little higher up, could be dried out.
SKY	I don't remember all this!
JOE	The farm is spread out, like. There, that was peas and oats. We grow 'em together. The peas climb the oats.
SKY	Cool.
JOE	There's your wheat, right up to those bluffs.
SKY	Wow.
JOE	Barley down on that side. Already in the bin.
SKY	The farm has really grown.
JOE	Everything grows, if it's living.

Beat.

SKY	What's that?

JOE	That's your canola.
SKY	I missed the yellow.
JOE	Swathed it before all that rain. Pods gotta cure. Gonna need about five dry days.
SKY	The colour of happiness.

Beat.

JOE	Wish your dad woulda seen it that way. His sadness was so foreign.
SKY	I went to see him a few times. I skipped school and took the subway to that awful men's hostel.
JOE	The only one who could light him up was you.

Beat.

JOE	Wish I could trade you for that.
SKY	You can't. . . . But I owe you! And one day, I'm going to pay you back.
JOE	No, I won't allow it.
SKY	But it was a lot.
JOE	You did all the work.
SKY	Why did you put me through law school but not help him?
JOE	I knew what to do for you. Just like I know farming.

Beat.

JOE	I live close to life. I grow my own seed. I work near the animals, and the birds. They tell me when a storm is coming, by how they move. The hand of nature pushes me, always, to get the jobs done that need doing. I fix machines, keep the equipment running. For the promise I make to the seed. I'm a part of all this, an old guy like me. Suits me right down to the ground.

Joe carries Sky's suitcases off.

SCENE 3   Candlelight Supper

Music. Mindy holds a lit candle in the darkness. Sky lights another from Mindy's.

SKY   These are gorgeous. They look brand-new.

MINDY   They were a present from your mother.

SKY   Oh.

MINDY   We haven't had occasion to use them.

SKY   Candlelight is centering, don't you think?

MINDY   Sure. Huh!

Joe enters.

JOE   We got a power failure?

MINDY   No. Candlelight, for a change.

JOE   Candles!

MINDY   Sky wants to set a mood —

JOE   Cause a fire!

MINDY   Make it romantic like. Huh!

SKY   I better check the lentils.

Sky exits, giving Joe her candle.

JOE   What's that smell?

MINDY   Spices, Joe. Sky brought her own.

JOE   I hope this is not vegetarian.

MINDY   I made your meat, but Sky won't take it, so don't ask her.

Solo enters.

SOLO   You folks okay?

JOE   Hey, Solo! Get in here!

SOLO	The wind knock out your power?
MINDY	We're having candlelight.
SOLO	What the hell for?

Sky enters.

MINDY	Solo, you remember Sky.
SOLO	Hey. Cinnamon.
SKY	Solo.
SOLO	Heard you were back.
SKY	Oh, yeah?
SOLO	Took you long enough.
SKY	Ten years.
JOE	Sky's part of the crew.
SKY	Never stayed for harvest before.
SOLO	A rare woman does that kind of work.
MINDY	Because if we did, the men would expect it all the time. I, for one, have enough to do.
SOLO	Remember when I let you drive the tractor? You knocked me off!
SKY	I pulled you back on.
SOLO	Remember the dugout?
SKY	Never got you back for that.
SOLO	We were just kids.
JOE	Anyone giving you a hand?
SOLO	No. Not this year.
MINDY	Now, that's not right.
JOE	What about that friend of yours?
SOLO	He's a company man now.

Beat.

SKY	Hey. Sorry about your folks.
SOLO	Yeah. Sorry about your mom.
SKY	I didn't know where else to go.
SOLO	Me, too. For weeks after.
SKY	So now you do it all by yourself?
SOLO	Have to.
JOE	He's young!
SOLO	I've done it before. I can do it again.
JOE	You rest when it rains. Round the clock when it's dry. Right, Solo?
MINDY	That's how farmers get hurt, so rag tired!
SOLO	When I finish, I'll be over to help you.
MINDY	You count on having supper here, then, 'til we're all through.
SOLO	If it's no trouble.
MINDY	Another person, another potato!

Mindy hands her candle to Joe, exits.

SKY	I hope you like lentils.
SOLO	I grow them.
SKY	What kind?
SOLO	Red.
SKY	Tonight you're getting green.
SOLO	Smells like another world. I can hardly wait.
JOE	You sure got good-looking canola.
SOLO	Hope it counts up just as good.

JOE	That all from the seed I gave you?
SOLO	No. I bought this year.
JOE	Not much weed pressure.
SOLO	None.
JOE	Can I swap you for some?
SOLO	No kidding! I can't.
JOE	Why the hell not?
SOLO	My contract says I can't save or trade.
SKY	Your contract?
SOLO	Always something new.
JOE	Just because it's new, doesn't mean it's better.
SOLO	It's the future.
SKY	New seed?
SOLO	Yeah. My buddy sells it.
JOE	Why buy when mine is free?
SOLO	An experiment.
JOE	Expensive.
SOLO	Something my Dad wanted to try.
JOE	You've been busy spraying.
SOLO	That's the point.
JOE	I don't agree with it.
SOLO	I knew you'd say that.
JOE	It's the time in, time out —
SKY	Consistent application of work that makes a farm grow.
SOLO	Yeah, well, you never wanted to trade before.

Sound of the wind.
Mindy enters.

MINDY	Ready, everyone? Oh, listen to that wind!
JOE	A two-bit wind.
SKY	Dad used to say that.
JOE	When he was little, I'd tell him to go out and see if the wind could lift a quarter off the ground.
SKY	He was afraid of the wind.

Beat.

MINDY	Come on, everyone, let's eat.

Mindy starts to exit with Solo and Sky.

MINDY	Kind heaven, speed the plough!
	And bless the hands that guide it.
	God gives the seed.
	The bread we need,
	our labour must provide it.

Joe blows out the candles.

JOE	I'm turning the lights back on.

Joe exits. Music.

SCENE 4   Apron of Many Pockets

Music. Mindy has a stalk of ripe canola pods. Solo waits with her.

SOLO	What's keeping them?
MINDY	Joe's not moving any faster these days.
SOLO	Harvest is no time to be waiting.
MINDY	Oh, yes it is. I had to wait 'til after harvest to get married.

Beat.

SOLO	How long you think she's here for?
MINDY	Our party is five weeks away.
SOLO	City girls, you never know.
MINDY	I came from the city. Bet you never knew that.
SOLO	What city?
MINDY	Red Deer, Alberta.
SOLO	Wasn't a city then.
MINDY	It is now.
SOLO	Not like Toronto.
MINDY	I'm still pinching myself that she's here.
SOLO	Looks like I hurried over for nothing.

Beat.

MINDY	Amazing what you get from one single canola plant. About thirty seeds to a pod, at least three hundred pods to a plant, that's nine thousand seeds! And you take one pound of seed, grow it out, and clean it, you get five hundred pounds!
SOLO	No one cleans their own anymore.
MINDY	I do.
SOLO	You can't get all the weed seeds.
MINDY	There aren't many to begin with. Not even wild mustard.
SOLO	You still got your share of Canada thistle.
MINDY	Everyone does. The scourge of the prairie.
SOLO	You can spray Canada thistle.
MINDY	I let it live on the edge of the fields to feed the birds.
SOLO	See, now —
MINDY	The birds live here, too.

SOLO	You get control —
MINDY	I don't control. I take care.

Mindy holds out some seeds for Solo to inspect, then pockets them.

MINDY	I hear you've got something new.
SOLO	Yeah. I like it a lot.
MINDY	What do you like about it?
SOLO	No weeds. Higher yield.
MINDY	How many times do you spray?
SOLO	Twice. It depends.
MINDY	That's a lot of fuel!
SOLO	I get a clean field.
MINDY	Hope you never spray on a windy day.
SOLO	No, M'am.
MINDY	Keep it on your side, Solo. Because the wind won't abide secrets. Sure as the lines on my face.
SOLO	This year's crop was my best so far.
MINDY	I think ours is just as good.
SOLO	I need to be sure. I can't afford otherwise.
MINDY	That's what they teach now? Up at the university?
SOLO	Darn right.
MINDY	No hoping or praying. Or trusting that the hand of nature is gentle and kind.
SOLO	I know better.
MINDY	Now, Solo.
SOLO	Nature and God and all that? I'm not losing out again. No way.
MINDY	But Solo, you're a farmer. You can't make Nature your enemy.

SOLO	If I was home that night, that storm would have killed me, too.
MINDY	Solo. It was a freak storm. Shows how powerless we are.
SOLO	I'm making all the profit I can. That's efficiency. That's growth.
MINDY	Solo. Do you want to be alone on this earth?

Beat.

MINDY	Remember. You reap what you sow.
SOLO	That's how I'm going to get what's mine.

Sound of the wind, whistling.

MINDY	You, of all people, should listen to the wind.
SOLO	What the hell for?

Beat.

MINDY	Now, that's strange.
SOLO	Where in the world are they?
MINDY	Look here. Joe sprayed over a week ago. But there's canola right up to the pole!
SOLO	That's what she looks like, green and growing through the weed kill.
MINDY	This is the new seed.
SOLO	You got some volunteers!
MINDY	This is from you?
SOLO	There they are! About time!

Joe and Sky enter.

MINDY	From that field, across the road?
SOLO	I'm the first guy around here to grow it.

MINDY	I gotta tell Joe!
SOLO	Hey, Sky!
MINDY	Oh, Joe!
JOE	What's the matter?
MINDY	Look. Here.
JOE	Second time I sprayed it.
MINDY	What?
JOE	Can't get rid of it.
MINDY	You didn't tell me!
JOE	Nothing you can do.
MINDY	Is this in our field, too?
JOE	Nothing I can do.
SOLO	Isn't it amazing?
SKY	Everything else is dead.
SOLO	Except my canola!
SKY	How?
SOLO	They shoot in a new gene, from a bacteria! Keeps it alive!
SKY	This is "the future"?
SOLO	I'm betting on it.
SKY	But it spreads.
JOE	Pollen travels like that cloud up there.
MINDY	Riding on the wind!
JOE	We used to call this rapeseed. It's a weed in itself.
MINDY	Now it's a weed you can't spray!
SKY	What do we do?
SOLO	Bring it in!
JOE	We won't harvest the ditch crop this year. We'll bundle it and burn it.

SKY	How far up does it go?
JOE	Can't see a difference at all.
MINDY	Did you hope I wouldn't notice?
SKY	Maybe you should test it.
JOE	If it's in this field, it's in the wind, and it's everywhere.
MINDY	Our pure crop!
SOLO	It's just enhanced.
JOE	Let's get going.
SKY	I'll get the truck.
SOLO	I'll get my rig, too.

Joe exits.

MINDY	Joe, wait for me!
SKY	Are you helping, Grandma?
MINDY	I gotta talk to Joe!
SOLO	Should I start at this end?
MINDY	I don't know what you should do!

Mindy exits.
Solo and Sky watch Mindy go, then look at each other.
Sky exits. Solo is alone for a beat. Music.

SCENE 5   Beer Buddies

Tyler offers Solo a beer on a full moonlit night.

SOLO	Did you guys ever think of this?
TYLER	So Farmer Joe's got our genetics in his crop.
SOLO	All I know is he didn't put them there.
TYLER	Doesn't matter. I just gotta make a report. And you get this.

Tyler gives Solo a leather jacket.

SOLO   What's this for?

TYLER   Comes with your phone call.

Solo puts on the jacket. It looks great on him.

SOLO   Does it fit okay?

TYLER   The company says happy farming.

SOLO   I don't want Joe getting any flak.

TYLER   Joe? There might even be something in it for him.

SOLO   Like what?

TYLER   Did he ever give you any of his?

SOLO   Joe's the canola king.

TYLER   You got any leftover from last year?

SOLO   Didn't use it all, because I bought from you.

TYLER   I hear it's pretty good against blackleg. Clubroot, too.

SOLO   Yup, disease-free. But yours is weed-free.

TYLER   Yeah, see? We might be able to do a little tie-in.

SOLO   That would be taking what's his.

TYLER   He brown-bags it out anyway, right? And our lab docs
          are wicked at combining stuff. I mean, disease-free,
          weed-free, all we need now is drought-free.

SOLO   Frost-free.

TYLER   Storm-free.

SOLO   Yeah.

TYLER   Sorry.

Sound of coyotes.

TYLER   Storm of the century.

Beat.

TYLER	I remember after, the moon hung down just like that. Quiet. Except for the flippin' coyotes.
SOLO	And me with a hammer, boarding up windows, and you in your work gloves, sweeping up glass. Ha! I didn't even know you had work gloves.
TYLER	Your folks let me hang out right through high school, no questions asked.
SOLO	We cursed the universe.
TYLER	When the sun came up we went fishing. Then got started on the harvest.
SOLO	What was left of it. Haven't been fishing since.
TYLER	No way! Two years? That's before I got the job.
SOLO	Who's got time for it anymore?
TYLER	Hey! How about this winter? Up north.
SOLO	Nah, I'll be driving all winter. Bills to pay.
TYLER	I'll do a promo deal with the company. We'll get a few new suckers, and show them how it's done, eh?
SOLO	Don't know if I can take the time off.
TYLER	All expenses paid.
SOLO	You can do that?
TYLER	When you get good yields you get the big fish.
SOLO	You're doing okay, then.
TYLER	You are. You got a pretty tidy return.
SOLO	How do you know?
TYLER	I checked.
SOLO	How'd you do that?
TYLER	A thing I got going with the fellas at the grain exchange.

SOLO	That's none of your business.
TYLER	Oh, but it is. You're my guy.
SOLO	You can't put your nose in my profit margin!
TYLER	I'm just making sure. That's all.
SOLO	Let me get this right. I'm performing for you?
TYLER	In spades, boy.
SOLO	Who's the customer here?
TYLER	I hand-picked you! Just in time, too.
SOLO	You don't get my numbers. That's not part of the deal.
TYLER	Hey, buds. You're a company man now.
SOLO	Get outta here.
TYLER	First, I'm gonna put my feet in Joe's field.

Sound of coyote choir.
Tyler whips out a Ziploc bag and finds his way in the dark to the pole.

SOLO	Ha. Hey Ty, hear that? Yip, yip, yip!
TYLER	Shut up!
SOLO	They're coming to get you!
TYLER	Stop it!
SOLO	Yippy yap, yap!
TYLER	Funny. By the pole, right?

Tyler takes his sample and exits.
Sky enters, with her own Ziploc bag.

SOLO	Yip, yippy, yip, yip, yay. Gonna eat you up! Yippy, yip-yip!
SKY	Uh, what are you doing?
SOLO	Singing to the coyotes.

Sound of the coyotes.

SKY	Do they do that a lot?
SOLO	Just special nights. Change of the season.
SKY	You know about coyotes.
SOLO	Oh, yeah.
SKY	What about the wind?
SOLO	What about the bank.
SKY	I heard.
SOLO	Joe and Mindy don't have to worry.
SKY	They're worried about you.
SOLO	I've got to use technology.
SKY	But aren't you playing with Nature?
SOLO	No. I'm working with it. A new way.
SKY	To get out of debt.
SOLO	To keep my farm.
SKY	And pass it on. To your kids.
SOLO	I'm a long way from that.
SKY	I know.

Beat.

SOLO	Joe and Mindy are all I've got.
SKY	Me, too.

Tyler enters and hides his Ziploc bag.

TYLER	Hey, Solo! Whoa, hey, hello!
SOLO	This is Tyler.
SKY	The salesman?

TYLER	Yeah.
SKY	I'm Sky.
TYLER	Haven't seen you in town.
SKY	I just got here, a few days ago.
SOLO	We've been working.
TYLER	Oh?
SOLO	Sky is Joe's granddaughter.
TYLER	Could've fooled me.
SOLO	Ty.
TYLER	So you're here looking for your roots.
SKY	I guess so.
TYLER	Black sheep of the family usually do.
SKY	Yeah?
TYLER	Takes one to know one.
SKY	Well. Good thing we're not plants, or you'd have to spray to tell us apart.
TYLER	A girl who gets chemicals!
SOLO	Hey —
SKY	I also get cross-pollination.
SOLO	Let's go, hey Tyler?
TYLER	The lady wants to discuss genetic drift! How about a brew?
SKY	I'm busy.
TYLER	Beer's like, organic.
SKY	I've got some digging to do.
TYLER	Hey, what have you got against me?
SKY	A degree in law.

Sky goes off to take specimens, taking out her own Ziploc bag.

SOLO	Time for you to disappear.
TYLER	So that's who this is about.
SOLO	Hands off.
TYLER	I didn't think it was Joe.
SOLO	Just leave her alone.
TYLER	A lawyer? Get real.
SOLO	Now. Before she gets back.
TYLER	What's she doing?
SOLO	Getting a sample.
TYLER	Yeah? Maybe I should get lost.
SOLO	Out of bounds.

Sound of the coyotes.

TYLER	Jacket looks good!

Tyler exits. Sky enters.

SKY	Solo? They're getting closer.
SOLO	Yeah. Cheering for us.
SKY	Us?
SOLO	For getting the harvest in.
SKY	Oh.

Sound of coyotes.

SOLO	They're just happy to be together.
SKY	Yeah?
SOLO	Yeah.
SKY	I'm not really a wild dog person.

SOLO	I'll walk you home.
SKY	Home. Huh. It got dark all of a sudden.
SOLO	Feel that air? First frost.
SKY	Smells almost sweet.
SOLO	Smells good to me only when it hits bare fields.
SKY	It's a lot colder than I thought.

Music. Solo takes off his jacket, and puts it around Sky's bare arms, and they exit.

SCENE 6   The Letter

Tyler pays a visit to Joe and Mindy. Mindy is in the yard. It's dusk.

TYLER	Hi, Mrs. Brandt!
MINDY	Is that Trudy's boy? How are you?
TYLER	Mighty fine.
MINDY	Have you gone out to see your mom lately?
TYLER	I visit when I can.
MINDY	And how is she?
TYLER	'Bout the same.
MINDY	You're all she's got, now.
TYLER	Don't I know it.
MINDY	Come and have some tea. There's pie.
TYLER	No, thank you. You've got company.
MINDY	Sky? Oh, she's family.

Joe enters.

JOE	Hey, big fella.
MINDY	Joe, remember Tyler?

JOE	Sure. Solo's friend.
TYLER	Yeah. Good to see you. Hey, is Sky home?
MINDY	She's out with Solo. I sent them up to the bluffs. How do you like your tea?
TYLER	Sorry, I can't stay.
JOE	I heard you're with that chemical outfit.
TYLER	I'm actually here on business.
JOE	Is this a sales call?
TYLER	You've been good to my mother, so I wanted to deliver this by hand.

Tyler holds out a letter.

MINDY	I'll wrap up some pie for you to take to her.

Mindy starts to exit. Joe takes the letter and opens it.

TYLER	Now, before you open that I just want to say —
JOE	Mindy?
TYLER	It doesn't have to go like this.
JOE	They're suing me!
MINDY	What for?
TYLER	I can explain.
JOE	Because their canola was in my ditch.
MINDY	That's ridiculous!
TYLER	It's just a formality, really —
MINDY	I should sue them!
TYLER	An offer to sign on —
JOE	You know I never bought from you.
TYLER	But we've got a contract with every farmer growing our seed.

JOE	Everybody knows I use farm-saved seed!
TYLER	But our genes are in your crop.
JOE	Says who?
TYLER	We tested it.
MINDY	That's trespassing!
TYLER	On the basis of what we found in the ditch —
JOE	Now look here, my friend. I don't spray my crop. I use a pre-emergent pellet. You can check that.
TYLER	We've got receipts from the input dealer saying you bought spray —
JOE	Just for my vegetation agreement. Around the power poles, like everybody else.
MINDY	We don't spray willy-nilly!
JOE	Makes a bad farmer look better.
TYLER	All our growers around here have signed.
MINDY	God help us.
TYLER	If you come on board, we'll rip that up and call it a day. And I'll throw in some complementary spray. Otherwise, you have to pay the royalty.
JOE	Fifteen dollars an acre? That's what Solo pays on top of seed?
MINDY	Merciful heaven.
JOE	They want their price on a thousand acres. That's fifteen thousand dollars!
TYLER	Farmers caught stateside are coughing up a hundred and fifteen dollars an acre. But for family friends . . .
MINDY	You sue us, then expect us to buy from you.
TYLER	I'm offering you a way out.
JOE	I'll do this my way.
MINDY	What do you think we're made of?

| TYLER | Our seed comes clean and pre-treated, on top of the technology. |
| JOE | I won't grow canola anymore. The land can lay waste. |

Joe crumples up the letter.

TYLER	It's too late for that, Joe.
MINDY	What do you mean?
TYLER	We believe you saved seed from last year —
MINDY	We always do!
TYLER	And used it this year. Knowing it was ours.
MINDY	How could it be yours?
TYLER	Because it tested out at sixty percent. Last year, it was thirty.
MINDY	Last year?
TYLER	Solo grew it two years —
MINDY	Two years!
TYLER	In a row. I bet Joe knows that. (*Pause*) Next year, it could be ninety percent. So you understand, you need to be on our contract.

Beat.

MINDY	I want you to go, Tyler.
TYLER	We'll talk again.
MINDY	Now!
TYLER	Think about my offer. (*Pause*) Tell Sky, sorry I missed her.

Tyler exits.

| MINDY | You've known for two years. |
| JOE | I should have talked to Solo. |

MINDY	You should have talked to me.
JOE	So I'm to blame?
MINDY	You're getting sued!
JOE	Because of Solo.
MINDY	Because of you. Not Solo.
JOE	Oh, you'll forgive him!
MINDY	I have to. So should you.
JOE	Not me. Not now.

Joe exits.

| MINDY | Where are you going? |

Sound of the wind, potent.

| MINDY | What are you going to sing now? Make sure he hears you! Loud and clear! Oh. Joe! |

Mindy is alone for a beat, then exits.

SCENE 7 Dream Bed

Solo and Sky make their way to an elevated area, looking over the land, at dusk.

SOLO	I only found it a couple of years ago. One of those days I'm wandering out here aching for spring. It's grown over with old brush . . . but these stones, smooth as skin, catch my eye.
SKY	What is this place?
SOLO	A dream bed. The Blackfoot carried up these stones. They'd lay alone, fasting and thirsting for days.
SKY	You can see all around.
SOLO	On this side, most of that land is Joe's. Right up to this bluff. There, mixed up with all that bush, into the hills,

	that's mine. Joe says, when you can see forever like this, you can see inside yourself.
SKY	What do you see?
SOLO	I see the land my father cleared, the sections I've opened up, and lots more to be done. Past, present, and future.
SKY	I can imagine it in ruffling waves of yellow and green.
SOLO	In this light, I see purple and red. Clouds are coming in. Changes colour again.
SKY	This is a lighthouse and that is a calm sea.
SOLO	You don't want to be up here in a bad wind.
SKY	It's quiet now.
SOLO	Not for long. Storm's rolling in.
SKY	The land looks at rest. Neat and tidy.
SOLO	Spent.
SKY	Shorn.
SOLO	Yeah. Shorn. And a little sad, too.
SKY	Why?
SOLO	Winter's coming. Creeping in, low and dark like those clouds.
SKY	I want to know about winter. My dad couldn't stand it, especially on the farm.
SOLO	Most people travel, to get away. Joe and Mindy used to. Joe said, to get an education.
SKY	What do you do?
SOLO	I have to work. Long hauls, mostly. I want to pick up a few courses, to finish, but so far, no time. . . . I play hockey. I play guitar.
SKY	And sing to the coyotes?
SOLO	Only ones who listen. Gotta do something or you go crazy. Crazy like a coyote.

SKY	Like my dad.
SOLO	I didn't mean —
SKY	Didn't matter where he was, he never fit in.
SOLO	What about you?
SKY	My mother was my anchor.
SOLO	And now?
SKY	I'm adrift.

Beat.

SKY	Do you know what happened with my dad?
SOLO	Joe never said.
SKY	They never spoke again.

Beat.

SKY	I thought it was because of me.
SOLO	Why?
SKY	I look like my mother?
SOLO	She was different.
SKY	She needed people, lots of people. She loved teaching. She loved an audience.
SOLO	She was beautiful.

Beat.

SKY	This is beautiful.

Beat.

SOLO	I haven't shown this to anyone.
SKY	Really?
SOLO	Except Mindy and Joe.

| SKY | Oh. |
| SOLO | Are they still worried, because of me? |

Beat.

SKY	They're anxious to get the lab results. To know how much their seed is changed.
SOLO	Is there something I should do?
SKY	Well, they've been saving for fifty years.
SOLO	So, what do I owe them?
SKY	I don't know. Fifty years of labour?
SOLO	Huh. Anything else?

Beat.

SKY	Their party is a few weeks away.
SOLO	And then it's winter. At least for me.
SKY	If you'll play for me, I've got a song.
SOLO	Like, a performance?
SKY	Yeah.
SOLO	You mean for the whole crowd?
SKY	Think of it as a gift.
SOLO	I'm a pretty private guitar player.
SKY	We could make it private.
SOLO	Just them.
SKY	And us.
SOLO	I only know three chords.
SKY	That's all you need.
SOLO	I don't know. I think I'll take the fifty years of labour.
SKY	I think they'd like this song. It's a bit different.

Beat.

SOLO	How does it go?
SKY (*sings*)	*Awake, O North Wind, and come thou South!*
	Blow upon my garden that its spices may flow out.
	Awake, O North Wind, and come thou South!
	Blow upon my garden that its spices may flow out.
	Blow upon my garden.
SOLO	What is that?
SKY	It's from the *Song of Songs*.
SOLO	Never heard of it.
SKY	They say it's by King Solomon.
SOLO	Oh, no.
SKY	Is that where your name comes from?
SOLO	Just call me Solo.
SKY	My parents used to play it sometimes, at weddings.
SOLO	We'd have to rehearse.
SKY	Tomorrow?
SOLO	Like every day. All day.
SKY	I'll bring lunch.

Beat.
Joe enters.

JOE	Who the hell do you think you are?
SKY	Grandpa!
JOE	You! First you tell them that my crop is contaminated.
SOLO	Whoa, Joe!
JOE	And this is the second year of it!
SKY	Two years!

SOLO	What's the difference?
JOE	Now they're after me to pay!
SKY	They're suing you?
SOLO	No way.
JOE	Intellectual property rights.
SKY	On the seed?
SOLO	They can do that?
JOE	It's their gene in the seed.
SKY	They own the patent on the gene.
SOLO	I paid the royalty.
JOE	On your side of the road.
SKY	They can't accuse you without proof!
JOE	They got proof! From him!
SOLO	Not me!
SKY	Tyler!
SOLO	For research!
JOE	What a sucker!
SOLO	I didn't know they would sue!
JOE	They want a fee on every acre! Fifteen dollars! Only a fool would pay that.
SOLO	I want a future.
JOE	I thought I taught you. I took up where your dad left off.
SOLO	I'm not getting left behind!
JOE	That stuff is gonna come and go to the border!
SOLO	No way.
JOE	Then, sure as shooting, across the bloody road!

Mindy enters.

SKY	(*To Solo*) What about neighbours?
JOE	What about friends?

The sound of the wind intensifies to the end of the scene.

SOLO	Tell me what I can do here. How can I help you out?
JOE	For starters, you can stay the hell away from my granddaughter!
SOLO	Joe!
SKY	Grandpa!
JOE	She's got a boyfriend.
SOLO	What?
SKY	I don't believe this.
JOE	Jeffrey, a big law professor in Toronto.
MINDY	What are you doing?
SOLO	You said you were alone.
SKY	I never said that!
SOLO	You didn't tell me about him!
SKY	I've got a life!
SOLO	In Toronto!
JOE	Get outta my sight!

Beat.

SOLO	You're on my land!
JOE	And you're all over mine.

Solo exits without looking back.

SKY	Solo!
MINDY	Joe Brandt!

JOE	I'm gonna ask Jeffrey to come out for a visit.
SKY	So you can embarrass me some more?
JOE	I want to talk to Jeffrey.
SKY	He's none of your business!
JOE	Get his professional opinion.
SKY	Who do you think you are?
JOE	They picked the wrong guy. I'm going to fight this. I don't care what it costs. All it takes is one farmer to stand up.
MINDY	Then you'll stand alone. Without me.

Beat.
Mindy exits.

JOE	Min.
JOE	Sky.
SKY	My dad told me to stay away from you! No wonder he cut himself off!

Sky starts to exit.

JOE	Don't go.
SKY	I was fourteen years old. We come up from the dugout, and he shoves us in the car in our wet bathing suits. Our stuff thrown in, bags spilling open. The car shoots gravel at Grandma! I see her fall! He screams at you for three hours until Mom gets him to pull over. The rest of the way to Toronto he won't talk. His eyes glaze over, like winter. We can't reach him. He goes every day, wandering, as if he is homeless. And then he was. I lost him. I lost you. I lost Grandma. I lost the farm. Mom had to work three jobs. Then he died. I sent you a map of where his ashes were because you didn't even say goodbye.
JOE	We did. After harvest.

SKY	You came?
JOE	You were away with Jeffrey.
SKY	Mom never told me.
JOE	Mindy and me, we walked that ravine. We went in together and came out scattered, like.

The wind intensifies.
Sky starts to exit again.

JOE	Sky? I need you here.

Joe is alone for a beat. Sky returns.

SKY	So I can pay you back. (*Pause*) It's going to storm. We have to find Grandma. Come on. Let's go!

Joe follows Sky. They exit. Wind roars.
Blackout. Music.
End of Act One.

ACT TWO
SCENE 1 Anniversary

Mindy is alone. Joe enters, getting ready for the party.

MINDY	After we drive Sky to the airport, I'm going to Regina with the girls and the kids.
JOE	The morning after our big day?
MINDY	Would have gone that night right then and there if it wasn't for Sky.
JOE	And the party.
MINDY	It's not a party.

Joe puts his pouch in his good jacket pocket.

JOE	It's for us.
MINDY	It isn't about us anymore.
JOE	How many are lucky enough to get to fifty years?
MINDY	And put the work of fifty years into a lawsuit!
JOE	That's why Sky set up the non-profit group.
MINDY	That's your sack of ashes, not mine. And not hers!
JOE	It's her present to us, for our anniversary!
MINDY	You're asking our guests to donate money!
JOE	People want to contribute.
MINDY	Who ever heard of raffle tickets at a fiftieth?
JOE	They do it, for a cause, in Toronto.
MINDY	It's crass!
JOE	Sky put a lot of effort into this.
MINDY	I've hardly seen her, with you two always at the lawyers'. I should have gone to Regina.

The Seed Savers, Workshop West Theatre: Maralyn Ryan as Mindy; John Wright as Joe. Photo by Russ Hewitt.

SKY	Sorry about rehearsal.
SOLO	You were busy.
SKY	In case I don't see you later tonight —
SOLO	You're dancing with me.
SKY	Then I won't say goodbye.

Beat.

SOLO	Will you come back for the trial?
SKY	I owe it to him. I should.
SOLO	Bring your skates.
SKY	I don't have any.
SOLO	You want to know winter, get skates.

Solo warms up on the guitar.
Joe and Mindy come out into the yard.

JOE	What's this about?
SKY	We've got a song for you.
MINDY	This is a surprise.
SOLO	It's a gift.
SKY	For you. For your fifty years.
MINDY	Another present!
SKY	Dad used to sing it. With Mom. So it's from him, too.

Sky cues Solo to start. He accompanies her.

SKY (*sings*) *Awake, O North wind, and come thou South!*
Blow upon my garden that its spices may flow out
Awake, O North wind, and come thou South!
Blow upon my garden.
Let my beloved come to his garden,
and eat its choicest fruits.

JOE	You had your baking.
MINDY	All for nothing.
JOE	You're tired.
MINDY	I'm tired of you, Joe Brandt, and I'm not going to your fundraiser!

Beat.

JOE	Remember when we almost got tractored out by the bank?
MINDY	The year Davey was born.
JOE	We recovered because of our own good seed.
MINDY	That seed is gone. Gone, like Davey.
JOE	Which is why I have to do this.
MINDY	Why, Joe. You threw it away. Like Davey. Then Solo. Now Sky.
JOE	No!
MINDY	I'm next.
JOE	If I can't save the seed that grows on my own land, then what?
MINDY	You're asking me?
JOE	I didn't ask for this. This thing chose me.
MINDY	Well, what if I choose, Joe. What then?
JOE	You might hold on to the house if you get rid of me.

Beat.

MINDY	Is that what you want?
JOE	I don't want to do this alone.

Solo, with his guitar, enters the yard with Sky.

SOLO	I said I would.
SKY	You don't have to, if you don't want to.
SOLO	Yeah, I do.

I come to my garden, my sister, my bride;
I gather my myrrh with my spice,
I eat my honeycomb with my honey,
I drink my wine with my milk.
This is my beloved and this is my friend.
Awake, O North Wind, and come thou South!
Blow upon my garden that its spices may flow out.
Awake, O North Wind, and come thou South!
Blow upon my garden.

MINDY   Is that your father's song?

SKY   No. I never found any of his.

MINDY   Neither did I.

SKY   I wanted him here.

MINDY   You bring him here for me.

Mindy hugs Sky.

MINDY   (*To Solo*) I didn't know you could play?

JOE   Who ever heard of wine with milk?

MINDY   It's a love song, Joe. You're the wine and I'm the milk.

JOE   Oh.

SOLO   I should go.

SKY   I'll go with you.

MINDY   Sky, wait.

SKY   Grandma, you better hurry up.

JOE   C'mon, Min.

MINDY   No.

JOE   It's time to go.

MINDY   I'm not going.

SKY   What's the matter?

JOE   She won't budge.

SKY	Solo, could you — go open the bar?
SOLO	I'll go open the bar.

Solo exits.

SKY	Grandma?
MINDY	I want to talk about Davey.
JOE	Folks are waiting for us.
MINDY	I've waited long enough. What did you say to him?
JOE	For crying out loud!
SKY	The day we left?
JOE	Not now!
MINDY	Sky is leaving tomorrow. And I'm not going any further with you, Joe Brandt, until I know.
SKY	Grandpa.
MINDY	Tell us what you did.
JOE	I didn't do anything.
MINDY	What did you tell him?
JOE	I told him to go.
MINDY	Because he wouldn't haul for you?
JOE	Because he couldn't! Harvest was early that year. Hot and dry. There was a demented wind. Davey was tormented by it. I shouldn't have asked him. I should have known. But I needed another hand. He wouldn't get in the truck. So I leave him standing in the yard, with his hands over his ears. I drive off, but I forget . . . my iced tea. So I circle back, and from the kitchen, I see him, in the yard, carrying all his papers, his drawings, his music, his poems. Then he crawls inside the haystack! And sets it on fire! I'm pulling him out, rolling him on the ground. He won't take my hand. His eyes are blazing at me! That's when I tell him. "Go. Get help in the city.

The sooner the better." Because I don't know what to do for him! I'm hosing out the flames and then I hear his car take off.

Beat.

MINDY	Oh, Davey.
JOE	I didn't tell you, for his sake.
MINDY	You saved him.
JOE	I didn't know we'd never see him again.
MINDY	(*To Sky*) Are you okay, dear?
SKY	He wouldn't talk about that day.
MINDY	I wouldn't have believed it.
JOE	And now?
MINDY	Now I know.
SKY	(*To Joe*) You were protecting me.
MINDY	And me.
SKY	And mom.
JOE	I didn't know any better.
SKY	No one did.

Beat.

JOE   I want you to be with me, Min. Tonight and tomorrow. (*Pause*) Are you with me?

MINDY   I've been with you fifty years. Fifty years tonight. (*Pause*) We'll see about tomorrow. Come on. I need help with my zipper.

Mindy and Joe exit.
Music.

The Seed Savers, Workshop West Theatre: Maralyn Ryan as Mindy; David MacInnis as Solo; John Wright as Joe; Natasha Napoleao as Sky. Photo by Russ Hewitt.

SCENE 2 Winter

Music intensifies. A winter wind. Snow falls.
Solo, at the dugout, shovels snow. Solo hears the sound of the coyotes, but he
doesn't call back to them.
Sky is in the kitchen. Joe sits. Mindy brings in some dough.

SKY	I came back from Toronto for that?
JOE	I'm not paying!
SKY	After a whole winter of work!
MINDY	Times like this, I make bread.
JOE	"No matter how it got there," the judge said.
MINDY	Nothing else will do.
SKY	"No matter how it got there! By seed spillage. Blown in by wind or by germination. From pollen carried by insects, birds, or the wind!"
MINDY	Now. You only need four things.
SKY	Four things.
MINDY	In ancient Egypt, they were female symbols.
JOE	Oh, Lord.
MINDY	The first thing is grain.
SKY	Flour?
MINDY	Before you grind it to flour.
SKY	We're using flour.
MINDY	Water.
SKY	Water. That's the next thing they'll want!
JOE	Put that judge on bread and water!
MINDY	Salt.
SKY	Salt of the earth!
MINDY	And yeast.
SKY	Yeast. I don't get it!

Mindy lets Sky knead the dough.

MINDY	Women hold the grain of life within them. Water and salt in the womb. And, like the pregnant belly grows, yeast makes the dough rise.
SKY	The ancient world wouldn't understand this ruling. Not patent law against farmers' rights. Not ownership of a life-giving form like a gene.
MINDY	Oh, those pharaohs, they thought they were gods. They owned everything, even people. Look at all those slaves who built the pyramids.
SKY	Can you own Nature?
JOE	Not in my book.
MINDY	We've got to have faith.
SKY	Faith in the system?
JOE	Faith in the seed.
MINDY	"For truly, I say to you, if you have faith as a grain of mustard seed, nothing will be impossible to you."
SKY	Patent law is federal.
MINDY	Oh, now, we've had enough of that. A whole winter, Sky.
SKY	If we apply now, the Supreme Court might hear it this fall.
MINDY	We've lost so much already.
JOE	It's not about us anymore.
SKY	There's really no other way.
MINDY	At his age, Joe should be fishing.
JOE	I'm not done yet!

Joe leaves the kitchen, goes to Solo, who is still shovelling.

SKY	Grandpa's tough. So are you.
MINDY	Me? Oh, I just want . . . spring.

Mindy exits.

SOLO	I'm taking her skating.
JOE	On thin ice.

Beat.

SOLO	I don't get why they didn't pay attention to the wind.
JOE	Why the hell didn't you?

Beat.

SOLO	They said you should have known.
JOE	That's between me and the telephone pole.

Beat.

SOLO	Woulda thought twice if I knew it would come to this.
JOE	You shoulda asked me.
SOLO	I don't need to ask your permission!
JOE	I wouldn't let you open the bag.
SOLO	Joe, I got the right to grow what I want.
JOE	You do. And so do I. That's why I'm going to the Supreme Court.
SOLO	No way.
JOE	They put a lien on my property. I can't borrow or sell or take any profit.
SOLO	You just have to pay up!
JOE	Not me.
SOLO	But Joe. You'll lose your farm.
JOE	Not if I win.
SOLO	How can you win?
JOE	I couldn't look Sky in the face if I didn't fight it. With everything I've got.
SOLO	Huh.

Mindy enters, uncovers bread.

MINDY	What will you do, Sky, if Joe goes to the Supreme Court?
SKY	The first thing is get him a new lawyer.
MINDY	That office needs more lawyers.
SKY	I mean, a specialist.
MINDY	What about Jeffrey?
SKY	Not Jeffrey.
MINDY	Oh?
SKY	Yeah . . . and he found me an articling position.
MINDY	When do you start?
SKY	Soon. But if there's a hearing . . .
MINDY	You'd stay?
SKY	I don't know.
MINDY	Well, then. That settles it.

Mindy and Sky leave the bread on the table and exit.
Solo, with his skates, and Joe make their way back to the house.

SOLO	You smell that? Fresh bread.
JOE	The woman's baking again.
SOLO	You're a lucky man.
JOE	Then you go in and tell her I'm going back to court.
SOLO	I'm right behind you.

Sky and Mindy exit with the bread.
Joe exits.

SCENE 3   Sales Call

Tyler is in his office. Music.

TYLER	Hey, dude.

SOLO	Hi. Good trip?
TYLER	Too bad you couldn't make it.
SOLO	How was the fishing?
TYLER	I dunno. I got kinda busy.
SOLO	With a girl?
TYLER	Yeah. Now she wants to move here!
SOLO	Huh.
TYLER	So how's it going with Sky girl?
SOLO	How do you think? She's pretty wound up.
TYLER	Who thought Joe would make it to the Supreme Court?
SOLO	Sky.
TYLER	At least you're making time with her.
SOLO	Not if I sign with you.
TYLER	What? You don't let a girl get in the way of your contract!
SOLO	I've got another chance here.
TYLER	Whoa, buddy.
SOLO	I gotta make it count.
TYLER	You'd chuck it all for her?
SOLO	To show her how I feel.
TYLER	Not like that!
SOLO	How do I make her stay?

Beat.

TYLER	You're seeding twenty percent more product this year. That's the plan.
SOLO	Yeah, but how can I?
TYLER	You wanna be like Joe?
SOLO	How do you mean?

TYLER	He's risking it all. To prove himself. To her!
SOLO	I just want to farm.

Tyler pushes the contract at Solo.

TYLER	This is what you do.
SOLO	What about Sky?
TYLER	Talk to her!
SOLO	What do I say?
TYLER	That's the fun part.
SOLO	Right.
TYLER	You'll figure it out.
SOLO	What happens when Joe loses?
TYLER	Forget Joe.
SOLO	I can't do this, man.
TYLER	You gotta save your ass, or you have nothing to offer her.
SOLO	That's the bottom line. (*Pause*) Give her here.

Solo signs the contract and pushes the contract at Tyler.

TYLER	Don't worry. Wait 'til she smells spring on the prairie.
SOLO	Spring. Can't get here fast enough.
TYLER	Take it slow.
SOLO	I gotta get to work. Driving to Calgary.
TYLER	Happy farming.
SOLO	Hey, I have to give this back.

Solo hands the leather jacket to Tyler.

TYLER	Go get her.

Tyler exits. Solo exits.

The Seed Savers, Workshop West Theatre: David MacInnis as Solo and Jesse Gervais as Tyler. Photo by Russ Hewitt.

SCENE 4   Planting Trees

Sky enters with a wheelbarrow full of bare-branched small saplings.
Sky starts planting the trees.
Solo enters.

SOLO	Taking a break from the file boxes?
SKY	I thought you'd be seeding.
SOLO	I saw your truck.
SKY	I'm making a windbreak.
SOLO	The wind comes from the northwest.

Solo changes the direction of her row.

SKY	I want to protect this field from that one.

Sky changes the row back.

SOLO	From mine.

Beat.

SKY	I hope I'm not too early. The nursery said as long as there's no more frost.
SOLO	You can tell by the smell of the earth.

Solo takes a handful and holds it up to her.

SKY	So that's spring.
SOLO	Like the scent of a newborn. Won't last. Next time, it's gone.
SKY	How do you know about babies?
SOLO	Calving.
SKY	Calving.

Sky and Solo keep planting, on either side of the trees.
Mindy and Joe bring a basket.

MINDY   What's she doing?

JOE   Can't build a fence high enough.

MINDY   She works without rest.

Beat.

JOE   Will she stay, Min? Will she stay for the farm?

MINDY   I know that a girl who comes from the city to work on a farm stays on the farm for a man.

JOE   So it depends on him?

MINDY   He works without reward.

JOE   That's up to her.

MINDY   No, Joe. It's up to you.

JOE   Me?

MINDY   To her, you matter like mountains.

Beat.

JOE   What about Jeffrey?

MINDY   Oh, Jeffrey.

JOE   Has he called lately?

MINDY   Oh, he's called.

JOE   You talked to him?

MINDY   When he calls, Sky's always busy!

JOE   Getting a little crafty now, aren't ya, Min?

MINDY   No use throwing fertilizer on that situation.

Beat.

JOE	She belongs here.
MINDY	And Solo?
JOE	She's the one fencing him out!
MINDY	Just don't you stand between them.

Beat.
Joe and Mindy exit.
Solo stops.

SOLO	Can we rest a bit?
SKY	You can.
SOLO	Have you got any water?
SKY	For the trees.
SOLO	Will you talk to me?

Beat.

SOLO	Why won't you see me?
SKY	I'm planting.

Beat.

SOLO	I'll let it go fallow.
SKY	So no canola.
SOLO	I'll rotate it further south.
SKY	It's already in the garden. It's going to come up here, too.
SOLO	Then I'll rogue it.
SKY	What?
SOLO	Pull it out.
SKY	By hand?
SOLO	You have to do it here, too. More than once.
SKY	Like, forever.

SOLO   I will if you will.

Beat.

SKY   Why should I throw my life away to pick your weeds?

SOLO   You left Jeffrey.

SKY   So?

SOLO   Why did you come back?

SKY   This place.

SOLO   Here.

SKY   I'm different here.

SOLO   I'm here.

SKY   This is not about you.

Beat.

SOLO   I waited all winter. I even read the *Song of Songs*.

SKY   I read files all winter. And now we have to go to Ottawa. But we could lose the farm! I lost this place once. Now I'm losing it again.

SOLO   No. Not if you're with me.

SKY   Because of you!

SOLO   Because of me.

Music.
Solo exits to the dream bed. Sky watches him go, then kicks over a sapling.
Joe enters.

JOE   In the country, you get to know yourself better. Sometimes, you're all you've got to rely on. But you need your friends, too. Huh. That's why your Grandma talks to the wind!

SKY   Wish I could do that.

JOE	Wish your father did. Might have saved him.
SKY	This wind never lets you go!
JOE	Best place for the wind is up on the dream bed.

Joe exits with the wheelbarrow.

SCENE 5 Desert

Sky makes her way up to the dream bed.

SOLO	You should go.
SKY	I should.
SOLO	Then, go.
SKY	I can't.
SOLO	Why?
SKY	Because I have lost my mother, and this is where my father came from.
SOLO	Then go to Egypt.
SKY	Why?
SOLO	Where your mother came from.
SKY	I can't go to Egypt.

Beat.

| SOLO | It's about as far away from me as you can get. |
| SKY | That's not what I want. |

Beat.

| SOLO | Then let me take you to Egypt in the winter. |
| SKY | Solo — |

SOLO	To know where the other part of you comes from.
SKY	I need to be here. Stand up to the wind, because Dad couldn't. Know how to be alone, because Mom didn't. Learn about happiness, what they never taught me. Why I love it here. Why I feel I'm home.
SOLO	Home.
SKY	I want a past, a present, and a future.

Beat.

SOLO	I know what you can do.
SKY	What?

Beat.

SOLO	Work Joe's farm.
SKY	Me? How?
SOLO	It's the work. Makes you part of all this.
SKY	But I'm not a farmer.
SOLO	It's in your blood.
SKY	There's so much to know!
SOLO	You'll figure it out. That's the fun part.
SKY	What about articling?
SOLO	Spring comes once a year.

Beat.

SKY	Teach me?
SOLO	Teach me about you?

Beat.

SKY	I will if you will.

Beat.

SOLO	You could put peas and oats there.
SKY	The peas climb the oats.
SOLO	There, lentils.
SKY	Green or red?
SOLO	Red.
SKY	Wheat?
SOLO	Hard red spring wheat.
SKY	Barley?
SOLO	Maybe.
SKY	I need some yellow.
SOLO	Mustard?
SKY	Mustard.
SOLO	Or if you want . . . I've got something old.
SKY	Is it a good yellow?
SOLO	It's pure. I saved it . . . for you.

Music. Solo exits. Sky goes to Joe.

SCENE 6   Truck Tour Two

Sky and Joe are in the truck, but this time Sky drives.

SKY	You can't just leave it.
JOE	Hell I can't.
SKY	There's still time.
JOE	I'm not working to hand it over to them.
SKY	Would you let me?

JOE	You?
SKY	Only what you think I can handle.
JOE	Son of a gun.
SKY	It would just be some seed.
JOE	Fuel, and fertilizer.
SKY	I'm paying. It's from Mom.

Beat.

JOE	Not canola.
SKY	Well . . .
JOE	What, then?
SKY	That field, wheat. Red hard spring wheat.
JOE	Hard red grows good there.
SKY	Hard red. And barley there.
JOE	No. Barley likes more moisture than you get there. Flax.
SKY	Okay. Flax.
JOE	What else?
SKY	What about lentils. Red lentils.
JOE	Good. And put some mustard in over there. For your yellow. Is that enough for ya?

Beat.

SKY	I'll try not to bother you. I can always ask Solo.
JOE	Yes, you can.

Beat.

SKY	If it fails, then who cares where it goes.
JOE	It won't fail.

Beat.

JOE	What about the city? Are you done with it, then?
SKY	I'm not my dad.

Music. Sky exits.

SCENE 7 Moving On Up

Solo meets Tyler in town, outside the bank.

TYLER	Hey, I've been looking all over town for you.
SOLO	I've been helping Sky open a new field up by the bluffs.
TYLER	Breaking new ground?
SOLO	Just trying something.
TYLER	So it's going okay.
SOLO	Ah, she's going soon.
TYLER	She's been going for a long time.
SOLO	After the hearing, back to Toronto.
TYLER	You gonna visit her?
SOLO	I don't know. All I know is farming.
TYLER	You'll know what to do. You're a smart farmer.
SOLO	I'd go bugs doing anything else.
TYLER	Someone's gotta feed the country.
SOLO	Feed the world.
TYLER	Keep me in business.
SOLO	Yeah, I heard!
TYLER	Why I love this place.
SOLO	Life on the farm.

TYLER	Everyone knows before it happens.
SOLO	Regional office?
TYLER	Winnipeg.
SOLO	Good for you.
TYLER	Hey, want to get some beer? Show me your little experiment?
SOLO	I should get going. She's waiting.
TYLER	If you go to Toronto, stop in the 'Peg, eh?
SOLO	Maybe.
TYLER	And when I'm back for my mom, you and me, we're going fishing.
SOLO	Yeah. See ya.
TYLER	So long, Solo.

Solo exits.
Mindy and Joe enter with shopping for their trip.

MINDY	Look, Joe.
TYLER	Hey, folks.
MINDY	Tyler.
TYLER	So. The Supreme Court of Canada.
MINDY	Nature is not for sale.
TYLER	You own the land.
MINDY	Nature will have her way.
TYLER	We're going to win.
MINDY	We'll see about that.
JOE	We have a right to grow what we want.
TYLER	What will make you a profit.
JOE	What grows best on our own land, from our best crops. The ancient right of farmers.

TYLER	The ancient right of business is pay for what you get.
JOE	Yeah. Heard you got transferred.
TYLER	Promoted.
JOE	Let me guess. Public relations.
TYLER	Yeah.
MINDY	Well, we're going on TV!
TYLER	Oh? I'll have to hear what you say about Sky's secret test plot.
JOE	What?
TYLER	Watch my smoke, old man.

Tyler exits. Mindy exits.

SCENE 8 Field Check

Joe and Solo go to the dream bed.

JOE	This better be good.
SOLO	You can see it from up here. There.
JOE	I told her no canola!
SOLO	This is yours, from before.
JOE	But they seized all mine! "Evidence!"
SOLO	You always gave me plenty.

Beat.

JOE	You can't certify it.
SOLO	That's not why we're doing it.
JOE	Huh. You won't get rich on romance.
SOLO	Romance. Huh.

JOE	What do you call it?
SOLO	Mending fences?
JOE	What if you get sued?
SOLO	We pre-tested the seed.
JOE	Think these bluffs will protect it, do ya?
SOLO	On the north. There's a wide fallow belt on the other sides. It's away from the roads. No canola for acres around.
JOE	Huh.
SOLO	Looks good, eh?
JOE	You put in some sulphur?
SOLO	Just like you.
JOE	You going to test it after?
SOLO	That's the plan.
JOE	Best cash crop I ever had.
SOLO	It likes the bush soil.
JOE	Mindy will like it, anyway.
SOLO	Don't tell her yet.
JOE	You trying to get me in trouble?
SOLO	Let's see how it grows out first.
JOE	Looks as good as it ever did.
SOLO	At least we'll know we've got it.
JOE	Huh. Better than the windbreak idea. But not much.

Joe exits.

SCENE 9 First Crop

Sky, with her suitcases, meets Solo in the yard. He has a bunch of wheat stalks for her. Sound of geese.

SOLO	So.
SKY	So?
SOLO	Ottawa.
SKY	Could be a landmark decision.
SOLO	I'll look after the farm.
SKY	It's goodbye to the farm.
SOLO	This is for you.

Solo gives her the wheat.

SKY	I'm going to miss harvest . . .
SOLO	Should be getting started right away.
SKY	. . . the sound of the wheat moving.
SOLO	I'll send you photos of the colours.
SKY	It's good, isn't it?
SOLO	It's excellent. You really get it. The work. The risk.
SKY	The time.
SOLO	I'll let you know about our canola.
SKY	My first crop.
SOLO	Stay in touch?

Joe and Mindy enter.

JOE	Well, this is it, for us.
MINDY	I just hope we have a house to come back to.
JOE	There could be a padlock on the door.

MINDY	Oh, don't.
JOE	A "for sale" sign in the yard.
MINDY	Don't say that!
JOE	Might have to move to Regina.
MINDY	Wouldn't be so bad.
JOE	We're two little round seeds, Min.
MINDY	As long as we're together.

Joe takes out his pouch.

JOE	This might be all that's left, in the end.

Joe tosses it in the air and catches it.

MINDY	Let's go. I can't look back. C'mon, Sky.
SKY	Wait. I'm an observer on this case. But it's my crop.
JOE	If we lose, it goes straight to hell.
SKY	It's my promise in that seed.
SOLO	Sky, let me do it for you.
SKY	It should be me.
SOLO	But it's the Supreme Court.
SKY	I need to be here.

Beat.

MINDY	We have to hang on to the farm, that's all there is to it!
JOE	(*To Sky*) You sure?
SKY	Yes!

Joe tosses the pouch to Solo.

JOE	I want you to keep this.

SOLO   With everything I've got.

Joe pats Solo on the back.

MINDY   (*To Solo*) Nature has us all in her hand.

Solo picks up the suitcases to follow Joe, but Joe takes the suitcases.

JOE   It's okay. You've got better things to do. Good luck.

SOLO   You, too.

Mindy and Joe exit.

SOLO   So.

SKY   So?

SOLO   Harvest.

SKY   Yeah.

SOLO   Anything else?

SKY   Maybe.

SOLO   Like what?

SKY   Feel like a walk?

SOLO   Where?

SKY   We haven't gone to the dream bed all summer.

SOLO   "O my Dove."

SKY   What's that?

SOLO   One of the *Songs*.

SKY   What's it about?

SOLO   It's about you.

SKY   Tell me.

SOLO   When we get there.

Sky takes Solo's hand.

SCENE 10 Supreme Court

Mindy and Joe are in the Winnipeg airport and look out at a TV monitor. Tyler checks the departures list.

TYLER	Gate 21. Delayed.
MINDY	Look, Joe! There we are again! Just like the wind! We're in two places at once.
JOE	You look . . . different, Min.
MINDY	It's all that makeup.
JOE	Look how they did your hair!
MINDY	You look good, too, Joe.
JOE (*v.o.*)	We gave up going to school to farm.
MINDY(*v.o.*)	A tough row to hoe, but we did it. So did everyone else.

Tyler spots Mindy and Joe.

TYLER	I guess I should congratulate you.

Beat.

MINDY	You go right ahead.
TYLER	Heard you didn't win, but you don't have to pay.
JOE	Not one red cent.
MINDY	Our farm is our farm. Our house is our house.
JOE	So how's Winnipeg?
TYLER	On my way to meetings in Toronto. Gonna call Sky.
MINDY	Oh?
TYLER	Next weekend, I fly to Chicago.
JOE	You just keep moving on up.
TYLER	You must be heading home for harvest.

JOE	Oh, we're not farming anymore!
MINDY	Heavens, no.
JOE	Not with the work laid out for us now.
MINDY	We're travelling again! Speaking engagements!
JOE	This winter, India and Thailand.
MINDY	Europe in the spring. All expenses paid!
JOE	Now, we gotta protect our wheat.
MINDY	Then there's my lawsuit. Did you hear about that?
TYLER	Don't think I did.
MINDY	I had that rogue canola hand-pulled from my organic garden. And sent the company the bill.
JOE	They refused to pay!
MINDY	So I'm suing them! For how it spreads!
JOE	That's my girl.
TYLER	Good luck with that.
JOE	Oh, look. I like this part.
MINDY	Oh, let's go, Joe.
JOE	Bye, son. Watch my smoke.

Mindy, Joe exit.
Tyler watches the monitor.

MINDY(*v.o.*)	The company is responsible. I can't let them get away with that. What would we say to our granddaughter?
JOE (*v.o.*)	She's a lawyer and a farmer. Just brought in her first harvest. Hi, Sky!
MINDY(*v.o.*)	We love you, Sky!
TYLER	Where's the bar?

Music.
Tyler exits.

EPILOGUE   Song of Songs

Mindy and Joe are on the dream bed.

JOE   Would you look at that.

MINDY   Is it the blue heron? Come to welcome us?

JOE   No, not the heron.

MINDY   What, then?

JOE   The bull found his way over the fence.

Sound of splashing, off, laughing.

MINDY   Cinnamon and salt!

JOE   Like a pair of otters. Makes me feel young again, healthy as a fish.

MINDY   Oh, Joe.

JOE   Heat steaming off 'em, splashin' to beat sixty.

MINDY   Let's go. Before they see us.

JOE   Remember when we used to do that? How 'bout a little swim?

MINDY   Go on with you.

JOE   Come on, Min.

MINDY   Hush, Joe!

JOE   Last one in is a rotten egg!

MINDY   Leave them be!

Beat.

JOE   As long as you hold on to me.

MINDY   Like the prairie holds down the hills.

Mindy and Joe hold on to each other.

JOE	Oh, look! Standing, on the point.
MINDY	There he is!
JOE	Hungry for his daily fish.
MINDY	Holding fast. Blue against the reeds.
JOE	Never get tired of that blue.
MINDY	Oh, I need it.
JOE	Looks like a king. Looking out for us, like.
MINDY	We're home, Joe. We're home.

Joe and Mindy watch the heron from the light of the sunset on the dream bed.
Sky and Solo enter.
Sound of wind.

SKY	"Set me as a seal upon your heart as a seal upon your arm for love is strong as death"
SOLO	"My beloved is mine
SKY	and I am his
SOLO	Until the day breathes
SKY	and the shadows flee."

Solo kisses Sky.
Sound of the wind, playful.
The far-off sound of a coyote.
Music. Fade to black.

Plays by Katherine Koller

Beatty. In *Instant Applause*. Toronto: Playwrights Canada Press, 2004.
Coal Valley: The Making of a Miner. In *The Alberta Advantage: An Anthology of Plays*. Ed. Anne Nothof. Toronto: Playwrights Canada Press, 2008.
Cowboy Boots and a Corsage. In *Taking the Stage: Selections from Plays by Canadian Women*. Ed. Cynthia Zimmerman. Toronto: Playwrights Canada Press, 1994. CBC radio broadcast, 1992.
Madonna of the Wilderness. In *Going It Alone: Plays by Women for Solo Performers*. Ed. Kit Brennan. Montreal: Nuage Editions, 1997.
Magpie. Toronto: Playwrights Union of Canada, 1998. CBC radio broadcast, 1995.
Perdu. In *10 Days of Madness*. Edmonton: University of Alberta Bookstore, 2007.
Starter Home. In *Three on the Boards*. Ed. Kit Brennan. Winnipeg: Signature Editions, 2007.